Married Women and Work

Married Women and Work

1957 and 1976

Alfreda P. Iglehart
The University of Michigan

LexingtonBooks
D.C. Heath and Company
Lexington, Massachusetts
Toronto

Library of Congress Cataloging in Publication Data

Iglehart, Alfreda P.
    Married women and work, 1957 and 1976.

    Bibliography: p.
    Includes index.
    1. Wives—Employment—United States. 2. Housewives—United States.
I. Title.
HD6055.I35   331.4'3'0973   78-75320
ISBN 0-669-02838-x

Published simultaneously in Canada

Printed in the United States of America

International Standard Book Number: 0-669-02838-x

Library of Congress Catalog Card Number: 78-75320

To Hari

Contents

List of Tables

Acknowledgments

A National Institute of Mental Health training program in mental health and sex roles (MH 14618) made the analyses reported here possible.

Thanks go to Elizabeth Douvan and Joseph Veroff for making the data available to me.

V. Lee Hamilton provided invaluable methodological and editing assistance. Yeheskel Hasenfeld and Gayl Ness made useful comments on earlier drafts of the book. I recognize the intellectual debt I owe these individuals.

Special words of appreciation go to Irwin Epstein and Rosemary Sarri for their countless suggestions, criticisms, and general observations, which enhanced the quality of the book. They stand out as my advisors, my mentors, and my friends.

A very unique expression of gratitude goes to Helen Marie Raef for the technical assistance and emotional support she so freely offered.

All the named persons share with me any credit this book may receive. I do, however, take sole responsibility for any deficiencies contained within these pages.

1 Changing Images of Wifehood: A Basis for Study

Most people would agree that times are changing. Certainly the popular press and television have done their share to recreate and review scenes from the American past. The fifties have been romanticized, and a poignant wave of nostalgia is now brought on by a pair of bobbysocks and penny loafers. This infatuation with the fifties frequently rests on selective recall that isolates only bits and pieces of that time period. Nevertheless, persons who have experienced the fifties, read about them, or researched them, have some sense that contemporary times are different in a number of ways. A discussion of these differences invariably includes a look at the narrowing gap between male and female roles. Societal norms governing appropriate sex-role behavior are not as restrictive as they once were.

Reactions to these changing times range from overwhelming acceptance to unquestionable repugnance. While debates persist on the merits and demerits of the fifties versus the seventies, the serious social consequences of changing times often go unrecognized. Definitions are changing. Role expectations are changing. The traditional gradually becomes nontraditional.

Women who hold roles that are being redefined deserve more attention. Housewives and employed wives can be counted among these women. Few scholars deal with the intrapersonal effects that normative changes can have on women. This is not surprising if one merely notes that women are usually studied vis-à-vis their relationships with men and children. Numerous studies have been generated that concentrate primarily on married women from this relational perspective. This book is not one of them. The goal here is to provide insight into the intrapersonal changes that may be occurring over time among wives whose roles have been, and may now be, challenged by shifts in sex-role ideology. Policymakers, social scientists, family counselors, wives, men—all people living in a changing time—should be interested in the following analysis.

Trends in the Labor-Force Participation
of Wives

The role of the American wife appears to be undergoing some type of change. Recent census data reflect the unprecedented number of wives and mothers who have traded their aprons for paychecks. This rise in the labor-force activity of wives marks the end of some rather long-standing trends. As a matter of fact, from 1900 to 1940, the pattern of wives' employment changed very little. Women worked until they married and had children, and the percentage of employed wives dropped with age.

World War II had a tremendous impact on the employment pattern of wives. Because of manpower shortage, great pressure was exerted to bring more women into the labor force. Women were encouraged to see work as part of their patriotic duty. Consequently, millions of wives marched from homes to jobs to meet the needs of war production. Few people were alarmed at the work activity of these wives and mothers. After all, a national crisis often required citizen involvement in some rather innovative and resourceful ways. Undoubtedly, most people assumed that after the war things would return to "normal," and wives would leave the work force to return to their usual place in the home. In fact, many wives did return home after the war, but many others continued to work.

Table 1-1 shows the labor force participation of women before, during and after World War II. The war years saw most groups

Table 1-1
Labor-Force Participation of Women in Various Marital Groups
before, during, and after World War II
(percent)

	All Women Workers			
Marital Status	*1940*	*1944*	*1947*	*1951*
Single	48	59	51	50
Married	17	26	21	27
Husband present	15	22	20	25
Husband absent	53	52	50	52
Widowed and divorced	32	36	35	36
All groups	27	35	30	32

Source: U.S. Department of Labor, Women's Bureau, *1952 Handbook of Facts on Women Workers,* Bulletin 242 (Washington, D.C.: Government Printing Office, 1952), p. 18.

increasing in their rate of labor-force participation. The percentage of married women, with husband present, increased from 15 in 1940 to 22 in 1944. After the war, this percentage declined to 20. Yet, this decline did not produce a rate that approximated the one of 1940. By 1951, the labor-force participation rate of married women surpassed that obtained during the war period. These trends suggest that a new pattern of normalcy was being established. Table 1-2 reflects the general rise in the labor force participation rate of women. In 1940, about 15 percent of wives (husband present) worked. By 1960, this figure rose to 31 percent, and in 1974 it was 43 percent. Waite (1976, p. 65) maintains that probably the single most dramatic and pervasive trend in the status of women since 1940 has been the increase in the proportion of married women who work for pay.

Another major deviation from an earlier trend is reflected in these increased work rates. According to Oppenheimer (1973, p. 185), the forties saw the entry or reentry of women past the age of thirty-five into the labor force- those whose children had reached school age. Figures from the Census Bureau (1973, p. 69) show that the difference between the 1940 and 1950 labor-force rates of wives between ages thirty-five and fifty-four represents the largest increase based on age for that decade. These figures reveal that, in 1940, 15.3 percent of the thirty five to forty-four age group and 11.1 of the forty-five to fifty-four age group worked. By 1950, the percents had

Table 1-2
Labor-Force Participation Rates of Women, by Marital Status, Selected Years, 1940-1974
(percent)

Marital Status	1940	1950	1960	1974
Single	48.1	50.5	44.1	57.2
Married	16.7	24.8	31.7	43.8
Husband present	14.7	23.8	30.5	43.0
Husband absent	53.4	47.4	51.8	55.2
Widowed	32.0[a]	36.0[a]	29.8	24.8
Divorced			71.6	72.9
Total	27.4	31.4	34.8	45.2

Source: U.S. Department of Labor, Women's Bureau, *1975 Handbook on Women Workers,* Bulletin 297 (Washington, D.C.: Government Printing Office, 1975), p. 18.
[a]Total percent for both widowed and divorced.

increased to 26.5 and 23.0, respectively. Thus, the pre-World War II pattern of a decline in the employment of older wives was no longer maintained.

With the 1950s, another pattern was broken. Oppenheimer (1973, p. 185) notes that there has been an increase in the labor-force participation of younger married women, including those with preschool children. Chafe (1976) also shares the view that, during the sixties and seventies, younger women of childbearing age show the greatest increase in the female labor force. At one time, this group was the least likely to seek employment. Van Dusen and Sheldon (1976, p. 112) observe that over a third of married women with preschool children are now in the labor force as contrasted with only 12 percent in 1950. Hedges (1970, p. 21) offers an overview of the employment of women, which indicates that black and immigrant women were pioneers, followed by young women and single women, then "mature women," and, currently, mothers of preschool children.

The employment rates indicate that women no longer relinquish the work role as they assume the spouse role. "I do" ceases to be associated with "I quit." Whereas it is plausible that the work activity of wives was destined to rise even in the absence of World War II, there is little doubt that the war years accelerated the process. Because the employment rates of wives never returned to "normal," a fertile area for economic and sociological analysis developed. Emerging trends become aberrations that needed to be identified, described, and interpreted. Consequently, much attention has been addressed to those factors alleged to be pushing and pulling wives into the labor market.

Wives' Employment: The Push and Pull Theories

Several perspectives can be applied to the study of those factors influencing the employment of wives. For the purpose of discussion, many of these perspectives can be subsumed under either a "push" orientation or a "pull' orientation. A number of researchers cite factors external to the household as responsible for the increase in employed wives. Based on this approach, it appears that wives are pulled from the home into the labor market. On the other hand, factors based on individual and household related characteristics have been pinpointed as encouraging wives to work. This area seems to suggest that wives are being pushed out of the home into the work force.

Prominent among the pull theories is the supply and demand argument. For example, Oppenheimer (1973) interprets the shifts in the employment patterns of wives in terms of labor market supply and demand. She maintains that employers preferred young and unmarried women workers and that, after 1940, the supply of these women declined. Oppenheimer goes on to add that it was only when married women with school-age children were added that a group large enough to cover the demands emerged. According to the U.S. Women's Bureau (1944, p. 17), the number of married women in the population increased markedly during the war years, while the number of single women declined. From 1940 to 1944, Bureau figures show that the proportion of married women in the entire female population rose by 8 or 9 percent, and the number of unmarried women fell 6 to 9 percent. This implies that married women were then needed to offset manpower shortages of the war years.

After the war, labor market conditions continued to be linked to increased employment among wives. Waite (1976) echoes the pull position by associating the rapid expansion of employment in "female" occupations (clerical, sales) with the rise in working wives. She notes that this expansion resulted in a demand for labor but that changing demographic patterns decreased the supply of young, unmarried women. Van Dusen and Sheldon (1976, p. 113) also assert that the post-World War II "baby boom" created a need for the expansion services (educational, medical, governmental, and recreational) in which most women workers were concentrated. Consequently, female labor was in great demand.

Certainly, this supply-and-demand explanation discounts and ignores any other shifts that may have taken place concurrently. The explanation is rather unidimensional and primarily highlights market conditions. The labor-force demands created a need for women workers. This view fails to offer any insight into the ways this demand was translated to wives (and husbands) to such an extent that wives were "compelled" to respond. The supply/demand factors may have indeed created the opportunity for wives' employment and, hence, exerted an influence with the potential of pulling wives into the labor market. It does, however, seem only logical to assume that other factors were also instrumental in motivating these wives to seek gainful employment.

One of these other factors may have been a changing political environment. The sixties saw an American society that was radically critiqued and dissected by a number of factions—many located on college campuses. In that era of politicization, the women's movement gained a new momentum. Polk (1972, p. 321) points out that, with the protest of the Miss America contest in Atlantic City in 1968, the Women's Liberation Movement burst onto the public consciousness. The Movement sought to erase the lines separating women's roles and duties from those of men. With the exception of biological differences (that should not be misconstrued as deficits), the Movement advocates that women and men should be treated as equals. Debates and arguments over role definitions, role inequality, and role expectations left the privacy of the home and moved to headlines of newspapers and covers of magazines. Women's role, place, and rights in society became a national political issue.

One major concern of the Movement is equal access to jobs outside the home for wives who want them. Occupational segregation, job discrimination, and income inequality rank high as issues demanding national attention and reform. Another concern related to the employment of mothers centers on the establishment of child-care facilities. Such facilities are invaluable resources for mothers with preschool children. A spotlight on these issues could have encouraged wives to consider labor-force participation as a viable option. In this manner, the Women's Movement can be perceived as a factor pulling women into the labor market. The force behind this factor is, of course, a much debated topic.

On the push side, several conditions are identified with wives' employment trends. The U.S. Women's Bureau (1975, p. 23) highlights such variables as wife's education, husband's income, and the presence (particularly the age) of children in the home. The last variable has been a major one affecting the employment of wives. Historically, the presence of a small child has had a powerful inhibiting effect on the work activity of the child's mother (Waite 1976, p. 74). Even though the labor-force participation of mothers with preschool children has risen dramatically, the presence of small children can and does affect the work status of the mother. According to the U.S. Bureau of the Census (1974a, p. 148), in 1970, labor-force participation was negatively related to the number of children and positively related to the age of the children in the home.

The relationship between mother's labor-force status and age of children could be interpreted to mean a mother accepts the assumption that her children require her presence full-time in the home. Imparting spiritual and social values to a budding human being may, in fact, be a twenty-four-hour-per-day job. This relationship could also mean that some mothers want to be in the home while their children are growing up. Perhaps for many women, fulfillment of the mother role precludes those activities that take them out of the home for extended periods of time.

The association between age of child and mother's employment status could also reflect on the absence of support structures needed to share child-care responsibilities with the mother. Hedges and Barnett (1972, p. 12) argue that the lack of child care facilities is a serious obstacle to the employment of women. Adequate child-care facilities would seem to make gainful employment a viable option for the mother of preschool children. In the past, this option did not exist. As child-care facilities increase in number, mothers may be able to enter the labor force with the knowledge that their child is in an environment geared to meet his or her needs.

The demographic shift toward smaller families, which affects the presence and age of children in the home, has reduced some of the inhibiting effects of children. A smaller family has the potential to "free" mothers for entry into the labor force. This conceptualization sees changing household composition as a force pushing wives out of the home. In addition, it appears that the presence of a preschool child is losing its negative impact on mothers' employment. Explanations of this weakening influence can often be couched in supply-and-demand terms. The demands of the labor market coupled with the decline in the usual supply of females may be great enough to override the inhibiting effects of young children.

Another push theory involves the role of labor-saving conveniences in decreasing the amount of time that has to be spent doing housework. Hayghe (1976), Kreps and Leaper (1976), Lebergott (1968), and Nye (1958) speak of the impact of technological change on the employment of wives. In the age of gilded gadgetry, wives perform household tasks in record time. The question then becomes a matter of occupying the resulting free time. Wives could devote more time to child care, to volunteer activities, or to employment opportunities outside the home. This free time hypothesis suggests that changes in household technology pushed wives into the job market.

The literature surrounding the role of labor-saving devices in shaping the employment trends of wives seems to embody an assumption that the home is the wife's top priority. This framework portrays work as something to fill (or kill) free time. It also deemphasizes any feelings of attachment a wife could have to working. The notion that wives enter the labor market because they now have the time to do so paints a picture of a wife who is basically uncommitted to work itself. Her home work still comes first, because it is only after its completion that she is thought to seek gainful employment.

Although these examples of push and pull theories identify different explanatory variables, most of them are guilty of using a biased frame of reference. They see wives as being pushed, pulled, forced, or otherwise compelled to enter the labor market. Underlying this orientation is the assumption that labor market work is not the legitimate work for wives. If it were indeed held to be a rightful activity for these women, then it would be nonsensical to speak of the forces that lured them out of the home. Approaches to the study of wives' employment often embody a hidden adherence to what can be called a traditional view of a woman's place. For instance, none of the major theories consider the possibility that wives could be developing a commitment to the philosophy of work. Rather, researchers adopted many of the premises, beliefs, and norms inherent in a specific cultural system. It now becomes necessary to delineate relevant aspects of traditional sex-role ideology that invaded the research responses to the increased work rates of wives.

A Woman's Place

A rise in the labor-force activity of wives challenges traditional sex-role norms that place women in the home—their work consisting primarily of unpaid homemaking and child-care activities. Ironically, recent labor-force rates for wives reestablish a tie with the economic world that was severed with the advent of the industrial revolution. Prior to the industrial revolution, economic activities were located in or near residences; this suggests that wives played an active role in providing for their families. As the workplace became separated from the homeplace, male and female domains were clearly established. Consequently, cultural norms governing traditional roles for the sexes were crystallized in the twentieth century.

Success in the female domain is usually associated with some very specific traits. According to Keller (1974, p. 417), core aspects of the female role stress nurturance; reliance on a male provider; concentration on marriage, home, and children; and a ban on expressions of assertion and aggression. Lifton (1964, p. 173) uses "passive," "small," "weak," and "soft" as characterizations usually associated with American women. These definitions and descriptions of "the" feminine nature have been greatly influenced by the female's childbearing potential. Mason, Czajka, and Arber (1976, p. 574) do suggest that the gender-based breadwinner-versus-homemaker specialization is often justified by beliefs about innate sex differences and the needs of children.

The home has stood out as establishing the boundaries of a woman's world. In this environment the woman was expected to find fulfillment and true happiness. The home offered a male provider on whom to depend, children to nurture, and housework activities to fill the day. Thus, this setting was an arena for the uninhibited expression of a feminine nature. A woman's natural and normal desire was so strongly confined to the home that, according to Laws (1971, p. 496), a woman who wished to give equal emphasis to some other area of concern was often seen as maladjusted, inadequate, immature, or in flight from her femininity. Housekeeping was every wife's career, and pressure was exerted to make sure women became housewives after marriage. Consequently, involvement in the labor force was heavily questioned.

It comes as no surprise that many theories of women and work reinforced these norms. Marriage and vocation were treated as incompatible. Women were postulated to become disinterested in work as they approached the altar. Many of these theories and norms found their way into the workplace. Employers automatically assumed that married women were uncommitted workers and frequently passed over them for the yet unmarried women. Work was just not expected or encouraged to be a core part of the lives of married women. Whatever intellectual productivity women possessed was thought to be realized through the wife and mother roles.

These images of American womanhood are more applicable to

white women. For this reason, traditional sex-role norms cannot be generalized to cover minority females. Many of these wives were allowed, and often encouraged, to deviate from existing norms. Historically, black and other minority wives have had a higher labor-force participation rate than nonminority wives. Because of the discrimination their husbands encounter in the labor force, black wives are more likely to assume financial responsibilities than their white counterparts. The employment of black wives mirrors a family adjustment to an oppressive economic structure.

King (1975, p. 119) holds that the housewife image and the sex roles associated with it in America do not reflect the reality of the black woman's experience. She agrees that black women have been forced by circumstances to contribute to the economic well-being of the family. Ladner (1972) asserts that the status of the black woman in America has been greatly influenced by African heritage, slavery, and the economic order that resulted from the Emancipation era. These factors have produced images of black womanhood that bear little similarity to the images of American womanhood. The usual cultural image of the black woman is that of a domineering, masculinized female (Staples 1973). Black women are also viewed as aggressive, independent, and morally loose (Ladner 1972).

It becomes apparent that the cultural norm placing women in the home is relevant for white women. Sex-role stereotypes are associated with Euro-American women, and these women are encouraged to adhere to traditional sex-typed behavior. A woman's place becomes more specifically the white woman's place. Yet, black wives' freedom to pursue gainful employment cannot be confused with liberation. Oppressive societal conditions often compel the black wife and, in some cases, the siblings to work as a means of maintaining the family.

While black wives are expected to digress from traditional norms, they are also penalized for this digression. Work rates of white wives have been usually treated as the norm for all wives. Hence, black wives are frequently said to be "overrepresented" in the labor force. Biases in the description and study of nonwhite characteristics are common, and the employment rate of black wives and mothers is handled as a social problem worthy of national attention.

Traces of the traditional view on the role and place of women can also be uncovered in studies of nonminority women and work. Kanter (1977b, p. 60) observes that, in research, the domination of this traditional view is reflected in a "social problem" orientation to women in the labor force. This means that research interests dwell on those aspects of women's work that have the potential for creating problems. Nevill and Damico (1975, p. 488) also assert that, whenever female multiple-role situations have been explored, the main concern has been with the conflict of employment and motherhood and the effect of this employment on variables such as family size, husband-wife relationships, and child development.

Numerous examples of this problem perspective abound in the literature. One popular research area has been concerned with testing the hypothesis that maternal employment was equated with maternal deprivation. A mother's "absenteeism" (resulting from her employment) was suspected to lead to stunted child development, loss of love, and neglected children. The relationship of mother's employment to the development, achievement motivation, self-esteem, self-concept, and delinquency of her offspring provided a pregnant research area (for examples, see Hoffman 1974; Hoffman and Nye 1974; Josselyn and Goldman, 1949; Nye 1958, Nye and Hoffman 1963; and Powell 1961; Siegel and Haas 1963; and Stolz 1960). Data generated from this volume of research are inconclusive and speculative. It is safe to say that no definitive results have emerged to prove that children of working and nonworking mothers differ on this social adjustment dimension.

Working wives were also thought to pose a threat to marital happiness and satisfaction, because power and authority traditionally held by the husband was thought to be shared with the wife if the husband were no longer the sole family provider. Numerous studies and essays addressing this issue can be found in the social science literature (for examples, see Blood 1965; Burke and Weir 1976; Clinch 1957; Day 1961; Durand 1946; Farmer and Bohn 1970; Locke and Mackenprang 1949; and Orden and Bradburn 1969). Hence, the cultural belief that a woman's world did and should consist of husband, children, and home was so pervasive that it permeated social science research—a domain often purported to be value free.

Wives and Employment: But What about the Wives?

Although working wives fell under the scrutiny of the researcher's eye, the intrapersonal effects of employment on wives have been practically ignored. The dearth of material in this area lends credence to the assertion that social research has been guided by a male-dominated perspective of women. Wives have emerged as important only through their wife, mother, and homemaker roles. Gainful employment became significant because of its potential for interfering with the successful execution of these roles.

Several studies can be identified that touch on the impact of employment on wives. An overview of these studies yields conflicting, confusing, and often vague results. Weiss and Samelson's research (1958) on 569 women showed that with marriage, housework tasks were referred to as providing a basis for feelings of worth by about 40 percent of working women and by almost 60 percent of the nonworking women. Feld (1963) found that employed mothers had more frequent doubts about their parental inadequacy. Nye's data (1963a) suggest that women employed full-time find more satisfaction in their work than nonemployed women find in housework. In a sample of working-class women, Ferree (1975) found that the woman who is a full-time homemaker is less likely to be satisfied with her life in general than those women who hold paid jobs.

Using data collected in 1972 and 1973, Weaver and Holmes (1975) did not find any significant difference in the work satisfaction of employed and nonemployed wives. In a study of 189 married couples, Burke and Weir (1976) found that working wives appeared to be in better physical and emotional health and held more positive attitudes toward life in general than nonworking wives.

What emerges from this overview is rather limited, sketchy insight into ways wives are affected by their employment, because studies focus on different aspects of the total picture. This is reflected in the dependent variables selected for investigation. As the dependent variable differs from study to study, it is difficult to pool research findings to make definitive statements. Frequently these reports use varying populations and methodologies, which also make comparability problematic.

A key drawback of these analyses lies in their snapshot orientation. Each study represents a snapshot taken at one point in time. The confusing results are inevitable if the effects of employment on wives are changing as society changes. Time frame is a paramount issue, because the normative structure is not constant. Since the time period under investigation incorporates the operative social norms, the meaning of employment to wives can vary according to the time of the survey. Hence, time can be a factor differentiating the ways wives are affected by their labor-force participation.

Studies undertaken during a more traditionally oriented period would be expected to produce findings that differ from those obtained today. Strict adherence to rigid sex-role definitions means that employment was not a legitimate activity for married women. The fifties have often been cited as a period in which traditional sex-role ideology received widespread support. Chafe (1972) provides a detailed survey of norms and beliefs of that decade. His report characterizes the fifties as a period marked by a resurgence of traditionalism in response to the upheaval of the war years. This suggests that, at a time when a record number of wives began entering the labor force, the norms of the day argued against their employment. Consequently, the trend toward increased employment among wives coupled with a greater sway toward traditionalism must have affected the lives of working wives. Komarovsky (1946, p. 184) observes that profound changes in the roles of women during the past century have been accompanied by innumerable contradictions and inconsistencies. These contradictions and inconsistencies paved the way for role conflict, social disapproval, or frustration for wives trapped by new situations that had not been defined or accepted by society.

For these individuals, several sources of conflict based on divided loyalties surfaced. According to traditional sex-role norms, this conflict was based primarily on feelings of dissatisfaction because of the time that was taken from the home. This conflict perspective saw the home as paramount in the lives of wives, and gainful employment was forced on working wives because of economic necessity. This conflict was eased somewhat because, through what was perceived as necessary employment, the wife was contributing to the well-being of the family. People assumed that her primary reason for working obviously was to ease some temporary family financial strain.

Another source of conflict could be found in what appears to be competing activities. The wife who wished to work outside the home probably felt that she should not do so. Friends, neighbors, and husband, as well as prevailing norms, said that she was rejecting her wifely duties by even thinking of taking a job. The wife who then elected to work no doubt had some ambivalent feelings because she was denied support in the pursuit of her employment interests. The working mother was in an unusually difficult position. Certainly work took her away from her children, and this work activity was thus frowned on by those around her. She may have felt that her place was truly with her children, so that being away from them was probably stressful.

The full-time housewife should not be overlooked. Changing

norms also affect her perceptions of the housewife role. During the fifties, housework had a greater potential for being a satisfying, rewarding activity. Through this role with its related activities, the housewife was carrying out her cultural mandate to give primary allegiance and total loyalty to her home and family responsibilities.

Changing norms, softening sex-role stereotypes, decreasing division of family labor by sex, more married women working, and a national political movement aimed at equality between the sexes appear to lead to a minimization of the stress and conflict experienced by the working wife. Yet, these same sources could also maximize the stress and conflict experienced by the full-time housewife. On the contemporary scene, as labor market work gains in its attraction for wives, housework may begin to lose some of its attraction.

These observations on the importance of time period form the basis for the hypothesis that the working wife of the seventies has more of a work commitment than did her counterpart in the fifties. The integration of work into the female role is more a product of contemporary times. It may now be more of a way of life rather than a stopgap to cover periods of economic crisis.

Burke and Weir (1976, p. 285) suggest that the contemporary wife who enters the work world appears to be expanding into a role that has more positive value for her. She sees employment as providing opportunities for accomplishment and creativity of a kind not possible in the home and for feeling useful and competent with respect to the larger social milieu. Through work, wives seem to be enhancing their personal growth and fulfillment.

Furthermore, the view of housework and the housewife role has changed over time. For today's wife, housework may be viewed more as a constraint. It probably does little to provide a sense of usefulness and importance.

Once, it seemed that the homemaker could derive usefulness and importance from immersing herself in such tasks as making beds, keeping a spotless kitchen, dusting furniture, and looking for her reflection in a squeaky-clean plate. Add to these activities the care and upbringing of children and it seems that the homemaker could enjoy a fulfilling existence. Now it looks like housework has lost some of its glamour and beauty. Much of the energy of some women's liberation groups has been directed to exposing the exploitation of women through unpaid work in the home. Even for women who do not agree with the movement's rhetoric, this denouncement of housework directs their attention to the negative aspects of their work.

In addition, for the working wife in the fifties, work was probably seen as interfering with the wife and/or mother roles. The wife-worker of the seventies, however, is expected to view her work as less of an intrusion and more as a welcomed role with positive results. The working wife of the fifties was more likely to have a negative self-image than the married working woman of the seventies. During the fifties, work had not been accepted as a part of the female role, whereas in the seventies we see less disfavor of married women working. Thus, in the fifties, the married woman's perception of self is seen as related to age of youngest child in the home, whereas in the seventies no relationship is expected between age of child and mother's self-perception.

In the fifties society dictated that a mother's place was in the home with her children, especially if they were young. The prevailing sentiment suggested that children needed full-time mothers to move successfully through the developmental stages of life. Although the biological umbilical cord is cut at birth, society refused to acknowledge this severance and persisted in tying the mother to the child. By spending time away from home (at work), a mother was thought to be depriving her child of the love, nurturance, and guidance needed for a healthy growing environment. During this period, a working mother with young children seems to have been justified in feeling guilty for being away from her children. However, in the seventies, the working mother appears to be emancipated from her children. Work is becoming a vital aspect of the female role, regardless of the parenthood status of the female. Societal norms governing a mother's behavior have eased somewhat. Around-the-clock presence of the mother in the home appears to be no longer a moral obligation. Because of the changing norms in the seventies, the working wife's perception of self is probably not related to the age of her youngest child.

The life of the working woman during the fifties is seen as less happy than that of the nonworking wife. The woman of the fifties probably felt that her energies should be directed totally to her home and children (if she had any). Work was a strain that drained her time from her real role in life. For the woman of the seventies, however, work offers a means of broadening her horizons and providing freedom from the "home trap." She is expected to emerge as being happier than the nonworking wife.

The Research

A 1957 national survey and its 1976 replication study provide an avenue for the exploration of these hypotheses. In 1957, a national study of mental health was undertaken by the Survey Research Center of The University of Michigan with the sponsorship of the Commission on Mental Illness and Health. This study is reported on in two major volumes, *Americans View Their Mental Health* (Gurin, Veroff, and Feld 1960) and *Marriage and Work in America* (Veroff and Feld 1970). In 1976, this mental health study was replicated with funding provided by the U.S. Public Health Service.

Both surveys study social adjustment and sources of well-being and discontent associated with marriage, parenthood, and work. In addition, self-perceptions (self-esteem, competency, identity) and coping styles were studied. The 1976 replication study was initiated as a means of investigating the social change that may have occurred in America during the nineteen years intervening between the study dates. The use of this replication data is one of the unique features of the present investigation. The two time periods are ideal for investigating the relationship between the social norms and wives' perceptions of the roles they occupy.

Data for these two studies were obtained through personal interviews with individuals, twenty-one years old or older, residing in private households in the coterminous United States. To assure the representatives of the samples selected in each survey years, area probability sampling was utilized. Hence, the individuals interviewed had the same characteristics as the total population. In 1957, a total of 2,460 persons were interviewed and 2,264 were interviewed in 1976. The respondents in both surveys were interviewed in their homes by a trained member of the Survey Research Center field staff.

Survey Research Center procedures were used for interview coding. Since translating the responses of open-ended questions into coding categories requires a good deal of inferential judgment, the investigators tried to ensure coding reliability by specifying in great detail what responses were to be considered under a given category

(Gurin et al. 1960, p. 11). The coding scheme developed for the 1957 survey was utilized for the coding of the 1976 survey. Because the sampling, interview, and coding procedures were identical, the comparability of the two surveys is not an issue.

Analysis and results use a subsample that consists of individuals who are female, white, currently married, and full-time at home or full-time in the labor market. Wives who are in the labor market part-time, nonwhite females, and single females are not included in the analysis. The 1957 subsample consists of 628 women who are full-time housewives and 149 who are full-time working wives. The 1976 subsample is composed of 337 wives who are full-time housewives and 231 who are working full-time out of the home.

Table 1-3 shows the employment status of white wives for 1957 and 1976. In 1957, 74 percent of the wives were full-time home-makers; by 1976 the percentage had decreased to 55. The percentage of wives participating full time in the labor force rose from 18 percent in the 1957 sample to 37 percent in the 1976 sample. In both years, 8 percent worked part-time. These figures suggest that more wives are working full-time in the labor force. Even though there is this sizable increase in the proportion of wives working full-time outside of the home, it should be noted that, in both 1957 and 1976, the majority of married women are working full-time inside the home. In 1950, 24 percent of the country's wives were working, whereas 43 percent were working in 1974 (U.S. Women's Bureau, 1975, p. 18). The combined figures for part-time and full-time workers in table 1-3 (26 percent in 1957 and 45 percent in 1976) are consistent with the national percentages.

Table 1-3
Distribution of Married Women by Employment Status for 1957 and 1976
(percent)

Status	1957 (n = 850)	1976 (n = 616)
Full-time in home	74	55
Full-time in labor market	18	37
Part-time in both	8	8
Total	100	100

Description of the Variables

Variables selected for this research are based on items asked in the 1957 survey and replicated in the 1976 survey. The selection of these items was designed to further minimize interpretational and comparability problems. Analysis chapters are based on a set of independent variables (demographic in nature) that are viewed to have an impact on the dependent variables (attitudinal in nature) under investigation. Each chapter emphasizes a different attitudinal dimension, whereas the demographic variables remain the same. Dependent variables are described in detail as they are presented in the following chapters. Demographic variables that appear to be correlates of the specific attitudes are selected for study in each chapter.

Inherent in the selection of demographic independent variables is the notion that attitudes are often influenced by structural positions. If attitudinal changes have occurred, it is important to know whether these changes are a result of wives' structural positions within society. Such an analysis plan allows for the study of the social underpinnings of wives' work-related and self-related attitudes.

In the analysis chapters, major emphasis is placed on the investigation of the bivariate relationships among the demographic and dependent variables. Tests of independence and measures of association, as well as the presentation of frequency tables, are used to describe and report these relationships. Kendall's tau-beta rank-order correlation is used. It is a measure of association used with ordinal scale data. It varies between -1.0 and $+1.0$ and is somewhat analogous to product-moment correlations (see Blalock 1972).

Researchers are generally confronted with the question as to whether the covariation in data is so slight as to be haphazard or so great as to be systematic (Winch and Campbell 1969, p. 143). Tests of statistical significance are often used to help answer this question. Statistically significant relationships are, of course, reported; however, the major goal of this research is not to uncover only those relationships that are significant in statistical terms.

Statistical significance is not synonymous with substantive significance (see Gold 1969). The researcher's theory and hypotheses often aid in determining substantially significant findings. Hence, relationships that are not statistically significant will be discussed when they appear to reflect trends in the data that may provide a broader base for evaluating the results. In these instances, the reader is urged to critically review these findings and decide their relevance and substantive significance.

The independent variables are all categorical. Interval scale variables (such as age and education) were reduced to sets of ordered categories. The categories themselves are important in providing useful information concerning social positioning. For this investigation, for example, it is more important to discuss educational attainment in terms of less than high school, high school completion, and some college or college completion rather than the exact number of years of schooling. Each category offers information about the degree of exposure persons within them have had to the influences and opportunities associated with levels of educational attainment. In addition, the establishment of categorical variables helps to remove the dilemma of having too few cases for analyses in some of the more specific study areas (especially those involving working mothers).

Age, education, occupation, family income, age of youngest child, and year of survey define the predictor variables selected for the research. The age variable has the following categories:

1. Twenty-one to twenty-four years;
2. Twenty-five to thirty-four years;
3. Thirty-five to forty-four years;
4. Forty-five to fifty-four years; and
5. Fifty-five years and over.

Obviously, one's place in the life cycle has a tremendous potential for shaping attitudes in a variety of spheres, work being only one. (Age of respondent and age of youngest child are highly correlated. Because of this correlation, age of youngest child is usually highlighted as the variable offering more information about the wife's family cycle positioning.)

Weil (1961), Orden and Bradburn (1969), Sweet (1973), Van Dusen and Sheldon (1976), among others, have noted that educational level is a factor influencing female participation in the labor force. Education may also be a factor influencing the wife's degree of attachment to her labor-market work or her housework. The educational system plays a major role in influencing the goals and expectations of individuals; it is also a major source of the contacts and training that will enable the individual to pursue those goals

(Van Dusen and Sheldon 1976, p. 197). The educational categories are:

1. less than high school (those who did not complete high school);
2. high school (those who completed high school and may have had no other schooling or other noncollege schooling); and
3. college (those who attended college or those who have a college degree).

The type of labor-market work one does certainly has a definite potential for shaping one's attitudes about work. Some occupations may involve setting and work tasks that generate positive work-related feelings. Conversely, other occupations may be of such a nature as to decrease positive work-oriented attitudes. In this research, occupations are grouped into four major categories:

1. laborers, service workers;
2. crafts, operatives;
3. clerical, sales; and
4. professionals, managers.

This categorization involves a rather global, simplistic ordering of occupations that is intended to provide a way of handling and conceptualizing, in a concise manner, the numerous occupational classifications. The 1970 Census Occupational Classification System was used as a guide, and the resulting occupation variable is used for 1957 and 1976 analysis.

Income poses a unique set of issues in this analysis. In 1957, respondents reported their total family income with no information obtained about their individual contribution to this income. In 1976, information was secured concerning total family income and individual earnings. For 1957 and 1976 analysis purposes, the income variable constructed here is based on total family income. In some respects, this family income variable serves as a proxy for the wife's income. It seems reasonable to assume that those families with wives making a sizable financial contribution will usually experience higher levels of total family income. Hence, total family income offers some (although rather limited) insight into the relative income of the wife. Obviously, there are problems contained in this conceptualization, and the utilization of this variable is undertaken with the recognition of these problems. Family income is categorized:

1. $0 to $2,999;
2. $3,000 to $5,999;
3. $6,000 to $9,999;
4. $10,000 to $14,999;
5. $15,000 or more.

Income categorizations were not the same in both surveys. The 1976 categories are more extensive while those for 1957 do not include expanded upper limits. The 1976 income variable could be categorized according to the 1957 variable. For this reason, the income variable used here is based on the 1957 groupings.

For across-year comparisons, 1957 and 1976 incomes are converted into comparable dollars based on Consumer Price Index (1967 = 100). Appendix A shows the 1957 and 1976 incomes falling into the low, medium, and high categorizations used.

The presence of young children in the home may also have an impact on the mother's work-related attitudes and perceptions. While attention has been focused on the degree to which children can determine a mother's potential for entering the labor market, the relationship of children to mother's feelings of work attachment has often gone overlooked. The mother of a preschooler may indeed perceive her true role as being in the home, caring for her child. Thus, she may not develop a strong sense of "connectedness" to her job or to work in general. For this reason, age of youngest child is viewed as an important demographic variable for the discussion of wives in the labor market. Age of youngest child is composed of four levels:

1. zero to five years;
2. six to twelve years;
3. thirteen to eighteen years;
4. nineteen years or over.

Appendix A compares the 1957 and 1976 wives by age, education, family income, age of youngest child, and occupation. These tables reflect some of the demographic shifts that have taken place across time.

Research Format

The analysis is reported in chapters 2-4 followed by a summary in chapter 5, which also addresses research implications. Initial analysis explores the across-time attitudes and perceptions that working wives have toward their employment. The goal here is to determine to what extent, if any, the meaning of work has changed for employed wives. Work satisfaction, work commitment, and work motivation are focal points for this part of the investigation.

All the wives in this research are considered to be involved in work, regardless of the location of the work inside or outside the home. Consequently, chapter 3 is devoted to housewives and their work. Attitude toward their work and plans to work (outside the home) are some of the study areas highlighted in the segment on housewives. This chapter also emphasizes across-time comparisons. The key question is: Have housewives changed or remained constant in their attitudes? This significant focus on housewives represents another unique feature of the analysis.

Chapter 4 seeks to determine the place of work in differentiating wives' perceptions of the wife and mother roles, their role performance, and their life happiness. Do employed and nonemployed wives have the same or divergent opinions on these dimensions? Has time affected their perceptions?

Results raise numerous crucial implications. Some deal with policy and intervention issues, whereas others concern the identification of areas commanding further study. Findings also offer a base for making observations about future trends, as will be seen in chapter 5.

2

Wives in the Labor
Market: 1957 and 1976

Public Attitudes toward Working Wives:
Then and Now

Although the labor-force participation rates reflect the work activity
of wives, these rates offer no insight regarding public sentiment. The
employment of wives has often been met with harsh criticism. In
recent years, much of this criticism is dissipating as the work rates of
wives continue to increase. A contrast of the contemporary social
environment with the one of twenty years ago reinforces the position
that attitudes toward the wife-worker role integration have experienced some change.

During the fifties, wives' employment was seen as synonymous
with the disintegration of the home. The ethos of the period is
captured in the writing of Lundberg and Farnham (1947). These
authors maintained that wives' work activity was a response to
masculine strivings. They also asserted that this "masculinization" of
women had serious, negative consequences for the home. According
to Friedan (1963), women's magazines supported the Lundberg and
Farnham premise by extolling the joys of femininity and family
togetherness.

Yet, the labor-force participation of wives continued to increase
despite public reaction against this trend. Chafe (1972) and Oppenheimer (1970) suggest that working wives coped with conflicts about
working by couching their motivation to work in purely economic
terms. Working to help send children through school, to help pay for
the car, or to help buy a house was certainly within the boundaries
of the wife's role as helpmate to the family—a view offered by Chafe
(1973, p. 21). Economic need was the socially acceptable reason for
motivating the wife to work. This position underscores the wife's
commitment to her family rather than to her job.

Indeed, numerous surveys found that the majority of respondents felt that it was all right for a married woman to work to
provide the necessities of living (see Glenn 1959; Nolan and Tuttle

1959). Hayghe (1976) and Sweet (1973) also used survey data from the fifties and sixties to report that economic motivation stood out as the reason most frequently given by wives for working. Oppenheimer (1970, p. 51) argues that, on the whole, people were not unqualifiedly enthusiastic about married women working outside the home, but if the goals were defined in an acceptable fashion (as really familial goals, for example, such as raising the family's level of living) and the opportunities for work existed, attitudes did permit married women to work.

More recent surveys reveal that public attitudes toward working wives are changing. Fewer people are disapproving of a married woman working even if she has a husband capable of supporting her (see Gallup 1972, and Tsuchigane and Dodge 1974). Mason, Czajka, and Arber (1976) review data from five sample surveys taken between 1964 and 1974. They conclude that women's attitudes about family and work roles are less traditional. In addition, these researchers also observed a sharp decline in the proportion of women believing that maternal employment is harmful to children's well-being.

Haber (1973), Hayghe (1976), U.S. Women's Bureau (1975), Van Dusen and Sheldon (1976), and Waite (1976) are among those who emphasize that, in the last decade or so, notions about appropriate activities and roles for men and women have become less rigid. It is apparent that specialization of labor within the family based on more traditional norms is in the process of change. Hayghe (1976, p. 14) and Miyahira (1975, p. 69) maintain that one sign of this change is less emphasis on the economic motive as the reason for the labor-force participation of wives.

Consequently, changing patterns of American family and work life are expected to be accompanied by changes in the attitudes employed wives have toward their job. A more supportive social environment does allow working wives to expand their roles to include work outside the home. Such a supportive environment may begin to encourage wives to develop and acknowledge a strong attachment to labor-force participation. Because of the changing social climate, the working wives of the fifties and seventies are expected to differ in their attitudes about their employment. This chapter tests for the presence of these hypothesized differences. The dimensions selected for comparisons are job satisfaction, preference for other work, and work commitment.

Job Satisfaction

Hypothesis: *The working wife of 1976 is more satisfied with her job than the working wife of 1957.*

The background presented suggests that the social climate of the fifties was void of substantial support for the working wife. Socialization processes as well as cultural mandates during this time dictated that the wife's self-worth was to be enhanced within the home sphere. Labor-market activity thus had the potential of generating role strain and role conflict. In the absence of needed social support, the working wife may have experienced some difficulty in viewing her job in a positive manner. The job itself may not have been the source of the problem, but, because it was associated with social disapproval, the working wife may have been inclined to see it in negative terms. In addition, the wife was not free to develop or express positive attitudes toward her labor force activity. The effects of this restrictive social climate are expected to be reflected in a lower percentage of wives expressing job satisfaction in 1957 than in 1976.

The dependent variable, job satisfaction, is based on the question: "Taking into consideration all things about your job, how satisfied or dissatisfied are you with it?" Responses were coded in terms of very satisfied or satisfied, neutral or ambivalent, and dissatisfied or very dissatisfied.

In surveying studies of job satisfaction, Kanter (1977a, p. 161) notes that, in a number of them, a surprisingly low percentage of workers express direct dissatisfaction. She also maintains that job satisfaction studies are based narrowly on just the job, its immediate setting, and its day-to-day comforts. These observations suggest that workers, in general, tend to say that they are satisfied with their jobs. This observation may be relevant to any analysis based on job satisfaction.

Table 2-1 shows the level of job satisfaction for working wives in 1957 and 1976. The 1957 and 1976 distributions are not significantly different from each other. The most impressive finding in the table is that more than 75 percent of the wives sampled in both years are satisfied with their jobs. The hypothesized effects of a nonsupportive social environment are not reflected in the data for 1957. Regardless of socialization processes, existing norms, and absent social supports,

Table 2-1
Job Satisfaction of Working Wives for 1957 and 1976
(percent)

Job Satisfaction	1957 (n = 149)	1976 (n = 231)
Satisfied with job	79	77
Neutral or ambivalent about job	13	11
Dissatisfied with job	8	12
Total	100	100
χ^2 probability	not significant	

79 percent of the working wives are satisfied with their jobs. In a social environment that appears to be more supportive of wives who work outside the home, an increase in job satisfaction is not observed among the 1976 wives.

Table 2-1 shows also that slightly more wives are dissatisfied with their jobs (12 percent) in 1976 than in 1957 (8 percent). With the current focus on hiring practices and sex-typing of jobs, working women may be more attuned to the negative features of their jobs and to the problems they encounter on the job.

The surveys used here polled wives at two very different times—times with contrasting social climates. Yet, the responses of the wives do not differ significantly. This raises a number of issues. First, the question itself may be tapping the wife's feeling about the specific job she has. She may respond by thinking of the work she does, the people with whom she works, her supervisor, the job setting, and other specific features (a point endorsed by Kanter 1977a). Obviously the frame of reference used by the respondent is undefined. Hence, the nonspecified referent could suggest that the measure of job satisfaction provides little or no real insight. Another view sees working wives as generally satisfied with their current job. In the fifties and in the seventies, working wives may welcome work as an opportunity to make money, to be out of the house, or to be involved with work associates.

Kanter (1977a) questions the validity of "job satisfaction" as it is usually measured, because a low percentage of workers express job dissatisfaction while a high percentage say they would seek another occupation if they had a chance. She suggests that other job preferences offer more insight into individual job attitudes than global satisfaction measures.

Preference for Housework or Another Job

Hypothesis 1: *The full-time housewife role is less desirable to the contemporary working wife.*

With the current emphasis on the importance of working, those contemporary wives in the labor force are not expected to see full-time housework as alluring or rewarding. In 1976, wives are freer to declare their allegiance to work. This view is gleaned from a survey of studies by Burke and Weir (1976), Ferree (1975), and Weaver and Holmes (1975), among others, that compare the position of the working wife with that of the housewife. For example, Ferree found that 53 percent of the employed wives studied thought they were better off than women who did not work.

Wives' other work preferences are based on the question: "Regardless of how much you like your job, is there any other kind of work you would rather be doing?" Responses were coded as yes, yes—mention of full-time housework, and no.

In table 2-2, the job preferences of working wives are given. In 1957, 22 percent of the working wives would rather be home on a full-time basis. For 1976, this percentage has dropped to 3 percent. Over half of the wives in both years do not prefer another type of job. Also, 41 percent of the wives in 1976 as compared to 24 percent in 1957 prefer some other type of work. The shift in the distribution of responses to this question is consistent with the hypothesis and Kanter's view (1977a) that other job preferences reveal more information about job attitudes than do global satisfaction measures. In 1976, working wives are less likely to say that they would rather be

Table 2-2
Working Wives' Preference for Other Work for 1957 and 1976
(percent)

Preference	1957 (n = 106)	1976 (n = 230)
Other work	24	41
Full-time housework	22	3
No other work	54	56
Total	100	100
x^2 probability	<.001 (x^2 = 40, df = 2)	

in the home full-time. This could indicate that they view their position in the labor force as better than the position in the home. In 1976, the wife's presence in the labor force seems to be based more on expressed choice than in 1957.

Rather than preferring full-time housework, more wives in the seventies desire another type of work (41 percent as compared with 24 percent in fifties). Education stands out as a factor likely to influence the contemporary wife's desire for another type of work. Education shapes individual goals, expectations, and aspirations. In addition, Mason et al. (1976) found higher education to be associated with less traditional outlooks, and Chafe (1972) noted that education was a critical variable fostering self-awareness among females. As issues related to women's place in occupational hierarchies receive more and more attention, better educated women may be more attuned to their specific job situation and the negative features of their jobs.

Yet, the effects of occupation on other job preferences cannot be overlooked. A contemporary wife in a higher occupational category may be less likely to prefer another type of work because of the positive aspects of her job (high pay, fringe benefits, autonomy, and so forth). Because better educated wives tend to be situated in better occupations (.41 correlation in 1957 and .49 correlation in 1976), it is necessary to look at the relationship of education to other job preferences while controlling for occupation. (Appendix B shows the separate relationships of education and occupation to other job preferences by year. An increase in the percentages preferring other work occurs at every educational and occupational level from 1957 to 1976.)

Hypothesis 2: *The contemporary better educated wife in a lower occupational level is more likely to prefer another type of work than a similar wife twenty years ago.*

Table 2-3 reports the results of other work preference by occupation and education. Although most of the cells in the table are too small to warrant comment, one of the more interesting findings appears among clerical and sales workers. (The cell sizes here are large enough to support discussion.) The college-educated workers in these occupations have increased dramatically in the percentage preferring another kind of work. In 1957, 36 percent preferred other work, whereas the 1976 percentage has skyrocketed to 63.

Several interpretations seem plausible. The characteristics associ-

Table 2-3
Preference for Other Work, Controlling for Occupation and
Education, 1957 and 1976

| | Percentage and Number Preferring Other Work[a] | | | |
| | 1957 | | 1976 | |
Occupation and Education	Percent	Number	Percent	Number
Laborers, service workers				
Less than high school	10	10	35	20
High school			25	16
College	50	2	33	3
Crafts, operatives				
Less than high school	17	12	23	13
High school	33	3	58	12
College			67	3
Clericals, sales				
Less than high school	36	14	33	6
High school	23	26	44	63
College	36	11	63	27
Professionals, managers				
Less than high school	17	6	50	4
High school	43	7	53	17
College	9	11	29	45

[a]Does not include those preferring to be full-time housewives.

ated with these jobs may be a source of concern. Szymanski (1974, p. 724) notes that compliance and meekness are important in lower level white-collar positions because these positions require the greatest subordination to the management. As women are generally concentrated in these lower white-collar positions, this compliance and meekness seem consistent with traditional sex-role expectations. For the contemporary college-educated woman, these required traits compounded by sex segregation on the job may be in direct opposition to a more egalitarian ideology. Hence, these women may be more likely to want another type of work.

For the modern day clerical or sales worker with some college education, a tendency to feel overqualified for the job may emerge. Awareness of this overqualification would be enhanced by the worker's educational level. Weaver (1977) found that, of all the workers he studied, women in clerical jobs were more likely to want to be promoted to something better; therefore, it seems reasonable that better educated women would have a much heightened awareness of the limitations of their job.

In the case of the college-educated clerical or sales worker, education and occupation appear out of step with each other. A similar case probably occurred twenty years ago, but it had not been identified, defined, or recognized as an issue commanding public attention. For the seventies, those women with less traditional outlooks, and in occupations requiring more traditional sex-role behavior, are the ones likely to prefer another type of work.

The increase in preference for another type of job and the corresponding decrease in desire for full-time housework could be a reflection of a greater attachment to work outside the home on the part of the employed wives of the seventies.

Work Commitment

Hypothesis: *The contemporary working wife has more of a noneconomic commitment to employment than her counterpart in the fifties.*

The measure of work commitment is taken from questions with slightly different wording. In 1957, this following question was asked of working women only: "If you did not need the money that you get from working, do you think you would work anyway?" In 1976, this following item was asked of all working persons: "If you did not have to work to make a living, do you think you would work anyway?" The researchers in 1957 did not think it was appropriate to imply that women could be working to make a living. They felt that such work behavior was more appropriate for males. In addition, there was some concern that women would be insulted if it were assumed that they needed to support themselves. In 1976, these issues were no longer crucial. This change in wording for working women could itself be a reflection of a changing view of sex-role behavior.

Although the questions differ somewhat, they will be used to determine across-time differences in wives' commitment to work. "Need the money" and "work to make a living" both imply a financial necessity to work. Basically, the questions seek to determine whether wives would continue to be employed in the absence of financial need. Those who respond "yes" are considered to be committed to work beyond economic incentives, and those who answer "no" are seen as committed to work for purely economic reasons.

Table 2-4
Type of Commitment of Working Wives, 1957 and 1976
(percent)

Type of Commitment	1957 (n = 107)	1976 (n = 227)
Noneconomic	58	82
Economic	42	18
Total	100	100
χ^2 probability	<.0001 $(\chi^2 = 20, df = 1)$	

Note: In 1957, several forms of the interview schedule were administered. One particular form (Form C) had questions omitted if the respondent were a woman. The skipped question pattern was designed to reduce interviewing time. Working women were of low priority, and some work-related questions were not asked them. The smaller number of cases for this particular item reflects this skip pattern.

Table 2-4 shows the type of work commitment expressed by wives across time. In 1957, 58 percent of the wives were motivated to work for noneconomic reasons as compared to 82 percent in 1976. This represents a statistically significant increase ($p < .0001$). The table reveals that contemporary working wives are more likely to be working for other than economic reasons. This absence of the purely economic incentive is interpreted to mean that these wives have a higher commitment to work itself or to their own self-realization than to just the financial rewards of working. Although work is a source of financial gain, the substantial increase in noneconomic work commitment does reflect the increasing value of other aspects of work. It should not be overlooked, however, that the noneconomic commitment to work was present among the 1957 wives to a degree that had not been expected.

For the wives working during a more traditional period, 42 percent seem to have been pressured into the labor market by economically based pressures. They do identify money as the primary reason for their labor-force participation. In a less traditional time, the purely economic incentive has declined drastically among working wives. To study aspects of this change in work commitment attitudes, the relationship of selected demographic variables to work commitment will be highlighted.

Education, family income, and age of youngest child are selected as the demographic variables to study here. Education and occupation are significantly correlated as are wife's age and the age of her youngest child (see appendix C). Education, rather than occupation, will be used, because it reflects exposure to and knowledge of the dominant culture and social structure. It is also a primary shaper of individual goals and aspirations. In addition, education is seen as a precursor of occupation. Hence, work commitment attitudes are seen here as a function of education: the wife's occupational level is viewed as a function of her educational attainment.

The age-of-youngest-child variable is selected here because of its potential for providing information about the wife's position in family life cycle. As childbearing and childrearing have often been cited as factors that inhibit the work activity of women, the development of noneconomic commitment to work may be related to the presence of younger children in the home.

Table 2-5 shows the correlation of work commitment with the demographic dimensions for the two periods studied. Across time, education, family income, and age of youngest child remain significantly correlated with work commitment in a positive direction. The higher the respondent's education, the more likely she is to say she would work even if there were no financial need. Education may instill values that support the meaningfulness of work for work's sake. Work may also be associated with achievement or accomplishment. The better-educated may be more likely to be motivated to achieve and to accomplish. Individuals with higher education may also have the type of jobs that reinforce their attachment to work itself.

As family income rises, wives are more likely to express a noneconomic motive to work. Those wives who do not need the money may be situated in families with high income levels. Their current work participation could already indicate their commitment

Table 2-5
Tau-Beta Correlations of Work Commitment with Demographic
Dimensions, 1957 and 1976

	Work Commitment	
Demographic Dimension	1957	1976
Education	.128[a]	.153[a]
Family income	.033	.106[a]
Age of youngest child	.147[a]	.109[a]

Note: Work commitment reflects economic/noneconomic dichotomy.
[a]Denotes statistical significance.

to work. Lower-income wives may be more likely to be working because of financial necessity. They are more likely not to work in the absence of these financial pressures. Family income includes the resources of other family members. A depressed family income may be associated with factors that would impede the development of a commitment to work, that is, low education, minimal job skills, poor job-related experiences, poor wages, etc.

The mother of older children may be free to develop ties to her job. Primary childbearing and childrearing activities have decreased for her. Conflicts over divided loyalties have lessened. Children are approaching or have approached an age that requires less mothering time. Younger children appear to be an impediment to the fostering of noneconomic work commitment. This appears in 1957 and 1976. It cannot be overlooked that younger children do demand more time, attention, and energy. The mother role may have more salience than the worker role especially in those circumstances that constantly remind the wife of her mother role. The presence of younger children may be such a reminder.

Shifts in the marginal distribution of persons falling within the demographic categories may have some influence on the observed increase in noneconomic work commitment among labor-market mothers. Since more wives in 1976 have higher education, higher family income, and older children, the rise in noneconomic work commitment may be attributable to demographic rather than ideological shifts. Bivariate relationships (controlling for year of survey) are studied to determine to what extent change in work commitment is associated with the wife's structural location along the demographic dimensions.

The relationship of age of youngest child to work commitment is found in table 2-6. At every age level, sizable increases have surfaced among those expressing a nonmonetary commitment to work. The largest increase is seen for mothers of preschoolers. In 1957, mothers of preschoolers had the lowest percentage expressing work commitment (31 percent). In 1976 this is still the case, but the percentage saying they would work even if they did not need to rose to 70 percent. A general shift seems to have taken place. The floor for work commitment for mothers in 1957 was 31 percent and now it is 70 percent. This lowest limit far exceeds the ceiling percentage of 60 percent given in 1957. The relationship of work commitment to age of youngest child still holds, but it operates at a much higher level.

Table 2-7 shows the types of work commitment by year and

Table 2-6
Type of Commitment by Age of Youngest Child, 1957 and 1976
(percent)

Age of Youngest Child *(years)*	Type of Commitment	1957	1976
0-5	Noneconomic	31	70
	Economic	69	30
	Total	100	100
	Number	13	43
	χ^2 probability	<.01	
		$(\chi^2 = 6, df = 1)$	
6-12	Noneconomic	55	81
	Economic	45	19
	Total	100	100
	Number	29	59
	χ^2 probability	<.01	
		$(\chi^2 = 7)$	
13-18	Noneconomic	57	82
	Economic	43	18
	Total	100	100
	Number	14	27
	χ^2 probability	not significant	
19 or older	Noneconomic	60	84
	Economic	40	16
	Total	100	100
	Number	25	44
	χ^2 probability	<.05	
		$(\chi^2 = 5)$	

educational level. Several points are worth discussing. Sizable increases in the percentage of wives expressing a noneconomic work commitment also occur at every educational level. The wives with less than a high school education increased by 17 percent, those with a high school education by 26 percent, and the college-educated by 14 percent. Regardless of education, more wives are reporting a noneconomic commitment to work in 1976. The largest increase occurs among the high-school-educated, and this increase is the only one statistically significant ($p < .01$). The smallest increase occurs among those with college education. This group had a high percentage of nonfinancially committed wives in 1957 (74 percent); hence, the potential for change in this category may not have been as great as the potential in the other educational levels.

Table 2-7
Type of Commitment by Year and Educational Level, 1957 and 1976
(percent)

Wife's Education	Type of Commitment	1957	1976
Less than high school	Noneconomic	53	70
	Economic	47	30
	Total	100	100
	Number	43	44
	x^2 probability	not significant	
High school	Noneconomic	55	81
	Economic	45	19
	Total	100	100
	Number	40	105
	x^2 probability	<.01	
		$(x^2 = 10, df = 1)$	
College	Noneconomic	74	88
	Economic	26	12
	Total	100	100
	Number	23	78
	x^2 probability	not significant	

In table 2-8, work commitment by family income can be observed for both years. Again, increases occur at every income level. The largest increase occurs among low-income wives, and the smallest occurs for middle-income wives. High-income wives rose significantly in the percentage committed to noneconomic incentives. Even in the presence of financial need (as exemplified by low family income), more low-income wives are also more committed to noneconomic motives to work in 1976 than in 1957.

Across time increases in the percentages of respondents expressing an attachment to work based on noneconomic motives are not associated with any particular position within the social structure. Observed changes are apparently pervasive, affecting wives regardless of their education, their family income, and the age of their youngest offspring. These findings mean that ideological shifts have occurred throughout the population—shifts that endorse the nonmonetary meaning that work is taking on for employed wives. For those persons who expressed a noneconomic commitment to work, a follow-up question was asked: "What would be your reasons for going on working?" Responses were coded in five general categories:

Table 2-8
Type of Commitment by Family Income, 1957 and 1976
(percent)

Family Income	Type of Commitment	1957	1976
Low	Noneconomic	33	76
	Economic	67	24
	Total	100	100
	Number	6	17
	x^2 probability[a]		
Middle	Noneconomic	63	75
	Economic	37	25
	Total	100	100
	Number	38	63
	x^2 probability	not significant	
High	Noneconomic	57	84
	Economic	43	16
	Total	100	100
	Number	61	141
	x^2 probability	.0001 ($x^2 = 17, df = 1$)	

[a]Not computed because of small number of cases.

1. extrinsic positive satisfaction (such as extra money or pleasant work place)
2. ego satisfactions (such as feelings of usefulness, being with people, chance to learn, liking to work)
3. work as habit (only way of life)
4. work as the proper state of things
5. work prevents negative states (responses such as "I'd go crazy if I didn't work," "Work fills otherwise empty time")

In looking at social change in a metropolitan community in 1956 and 1971, Duncan, Schuman, and Duncan (1973, pp. 22-23) found that the most frequently mentioned noneconomic reasons for women working were to get out of the house, boredom at home, or a dislike of housework. These reasons were cited for 1956 and 1971. If work is indeed becoming a vital aspect of the wife role, it seems logical to hypothesize that a higher percentage of contemporary wives will cite the meaningfulness and usefulness of work as the basis for their noneconomic work commitment. Work is expected to be seen as no longer just a means of avoiding boredom or getting out of the house.

The results in table 2-9 are consistent with the Duncan findings. In 1957, 52 percent of the wives who are committed to work say that work prevents some negative state or condition. (The following types of responses are more examples of those coded in this category: "Work is better than housework," "Work is better than staying home," "Work keeps me from thinking about my personal problems," and "I like to keep busy.") In 1976, "work prevents negative state" and "ego satisfactions" both have the highest percentages of responses (44 percent each). Work as "just something to do" is declining in importance among wives. The increase in the percentage offering ego satisfying reasons could reflect the added meaning that work is taking on for wives. Women are now identifying some of the ego-related motives for being committed to work for nonmonetary motives. Whereas work may be taking on an added dimension for some wives, a number of other wives are still defining work as a means of keeping busy and out of the house.

It is suspected that the incidence of ego-satisfying reasons is associated with educational level. Better-educated persons may be more attuned to identifying the intrinsically satisfying and gratifying aspects of employment. They may be more socialized to "be in touch" with their ego functioning and with the intangibles of life. In addition, a certain degree of articulation is required to communicate these ego-satisfying reasons to a listener. The tendency of the higher-educated women to be in more challenging jobs must not be overlooked, because a better work situation may provide more opportunities for ego satisfaction.

Consequently, the relationship of ego-based reasons for noneco-

Table 2-9
Reasons for Working in the Absence of Financial Need, 1957 and 1976
(percent)

Reasons for Working	1957 (n = 60)	1976 (n = 183)
Extra money	3	6
Ego satisfaction	33	44
Habit	8	2
Proper thing to do		4
Prevents negative state	52	44
Other reasons	3	
Total	100	100
χ^2 probability		.01
	$(\chi^2 = 17, df = 5)$	

nomic work commitment and educational level will be highlighted here. Table 2-10 shows a positive relationship between education and the offering of ego-related reasons. Whereas 37 percent of the college-educated liked the accomplishment and usefulness of working in 1957, this percentage rose sharply to 61 percent in 1976. This table shows that the increase in this category has taken place primarily among college-educated women. These persons are more likely to recognize and acknowledge the ego-rewarding aspects of working in 1976. The other educational levels have not changed in their percentages to the extent that the college-educated have.

Conclusions

Although 79 percent of the 1957 wives and 77 percent of the 1976 wives expressed satisfaction with their current job, the 1976 wives increased significantly the percentage preferring another type of work. Of the contemporary wives, 41 percent preferred another job as compared to 24 percent of the postwar wives. For the wives in the seventies, Kanter's observations (1977a) appear valid: a low percentage of workers express job dissatisfaction, while a sizable percentage prefer another occupation.

More contemporary wives are also expressing a noneconomic commitment to work. Each educational, family income, and youngest child's age level sees an increase in those wives committed to work for nonmonetary motives. Structural variables appear to only slightly differentiate the work commitment attitudes of wives. The

Table 2-10
Ego-Satisfaction as Reason for Working, by Education,
1957 and 1976
(percent)

	Wives Offering Ego Satisfaction as Reason for Working			
	1957		1976	
Education	Percent	Number	Percent	Number
Less than high school	30	23	38	29
High school	33	21	33	85
College	37	16	61	69

high-school-educated, those with low and high family income, and mothers of preschoolers have the largest significant increases in noneconomic work commitment.

Consequently, the time of the survey has surfaced as an extremely important factor in the study of the work-related attitudes of wives. The year variable covers a variety of aspects that are not reflected in education, family income, or age of youngest child. Time carries with it some information about the norms, beliefs, public opinions, books, movies, current events, etc., in a given social system. It represents all the influences existing that would inhibit or encourage a wife to seek and obtain gainful employment.

For the 22 percent of working wives who preferred to be in the home full-time in 1957, gainful employment was not a choice. These wives were caught in a period of transition. The transition seems almost complete by 1976 as only 3 percent of the working wives desire to be full-time housewives. The times are changing, with housewifery no longer considered attractive, desirable, or alluring by those wives in the labor force.

Another shift may be starting. An increase occurred among those wives stating ego-based reasons for their noneconomic commitment to work. A large number, however, still view work as a means of keeping them and their minds busy. The college-educated wives seem more likely to describe their work in ego-satisfying terms. These people may be forerunners in establishing work as a central avenue to self-actualization for working wives.

Whereas the proportion of wives who express a noneconomic commitment to work seems to be rising, it should not be overlooked that the majority of working wives in 1957 did indicate that they would continue to work in the absence of financial necessity. Even during a time when they received perhaps a minimum of encouragement to this type of commitment to work, some wives were, nonetheless, developing it.

3

Housewives and Their Work: 1957 and 1976

Housework: A New Social Disease?

During the seventies, housework and the role of housewife are being stigmatized as a new type of social disease. If there were a type of glamour or beauty associated with housework, this glamour and beauty have now been transformed into exploitation and dullness. The social milieu surrounding the contemporary housewife differs markedly from the one surrounding the housewife of twenty years ago.

The mass media were instrumental in supporting the traditional role of women in society during the fifties. Advertisers and women's magazines, according to Betty Friedan (1963), romanticized the housewife role and defined it as the ultimate in feminine fulfillment. Friedan also maintains that in the years after World War II, American women were the innocent prey of a "feminine mystique" that permeated society and located female happiness within the boundaries of the home.

Earlier studies show that housewives were finding satisfaction and fulfillment in their role. Weiss and Samelson (1958) found that housework tasks were referred to as providing a basis for feelings of worth by the majority of married women who were not gainfully employed. Nolan and Tuttle (1959) found that the advantages of full-time homemaking included "being own boss," "enjoying doing specific task," and "enjoying caring for family" for the sample of women they studied. Over half of the homemakers stated that there were no disadvantages to being a full-time homemaker. A 1950 poll revealed that 80 percent of the housewives surveyed received a lot or a fair amount of pleasure and satisfaction out of housework (Gallup 1972, p. 908).

Lopata (1971) looked at housewives living in Chicago suburbs during the late fifties. She conceptualized housework as one part of the housewife role, and the other aspects included the wife and mother roles. Lopata found that these housewives enjoyed their freedom from supervision and the interpersonal relations with their husbands and children. These results reinforce the view that, during the fifties, the majority of housewives apparently had some positive feelings about their work.

The upsurgence of the Women's Liberation Movement during the sixties raised questions about the lives of women. Housework, or unpaid labor in the home, became defined as exploitation (see Mainardi 1970, and O'Reilly 1973). Deckard (1975, p. 56), in writing about the Movement, provides a scathing critique of housework that could be offensive to any housewife. She argues that most housework consists of mopping floors, washing dishes, and cleaning toilet bowls—a perfect job for the feeble-minded. Deckard goes further to reveal that, in the expressive phrase of the Movement, housework is "shit work." Other rhetoric of the Movement has described housework as menial, dull, degrading, and humiliating.

Chafe (1972, p. 238) cites the most notable characteristic of the Movement as its ability to make the news. Networks and magazines carried to the public many of the issues underlying the feminine protest. The frustration of many women with domesticity was given nationwide exposure (see Chafe 1972, p. 239). In this manner, housewives became more aware of the controversy surrounding their "natural" place and role in the home. For some wives, the Movement served to foster a freedom to denounce traditional roles and choices. Perhaps these women had been fearful of social ostracism and, therefore, had not previously voiced any frustration. For other wives, the rhetoric of the Movement may have served to generate defensive feelings because of its wholesale attack of the housewife role.

Aspects of the literature emerging in the seventies appear to mirror a more negative orientation to housework. Oakley (1974) suggests that the characteristic features of the housewife role in modern industrialized society are: (1) its exclusive allocation to women; (2) its status as nonwork; (3) its association with economic dependence; and (4) its primacy to women, that is, its priority over other roles. She speaks of the "social trivialization of housework" because this work receives no pay, no benefits, and no status. Oakley maintains that housework cannot supply motivation or the means for self-actualization.

In reviewing the literature surrounding housework, Glazer (1977) maintains that many sociologists failed to recognize women's work— housework—as work. She attributes this major oversight to the nonmonetary status of housework. Her argument suggests that monetary and social rights seem to belong to those who are economically productive. Since women do not receive financial payment for their housework, they then appear not to be entitled to the same social and economic rights as those persons who are gainfully employed. Glazer reviews some of the issues related to housework and generally uses her analysis to criticize the role of the housewife from a number of perspectives.

In a study of working-class wives, Ferree (1975) found the wife with a full-time outside job felt herself to be better off than the full-time housewife. She traced housewives' dissatisfaction with housework to the low self-esteem, social isolation, and powerlessness it promoted. Miyahira (1975) observed that married women (as compared with single, separated, divorced, and widowed women) had higher expectations for labor-force work to be interesting and to provide social opportunities. She interpreted these results to reflect a desire for the stimulation and social interaction not found in the housewife's relatively isolated existence.

Two themes appear to be present in these contemporary discussions of housework. One has to do with society's devaluation of the "work" that women do in their homes. Their work receives no pay, recognition, status, or other benefits. This orientation seems to be an extension of the women-as-second-class-citizens concept. Because they do not have equality with men, women are thus relegated to a role that is primarily outside the mainstream of society. The low status of women seems to have been influential in the social trivialization of housework. The second theme has to do with the nature of the housework tasks. These tasks have been described as dull, meaningless, repetitive, monotonous, never-ending, and humiliating. The woman who performs them is thought to be powerless, socially isolated, and generally alienated. Because she is performing devalued functions, she is perceived as having low self-esteem, low motivation, and few opportunities to achieve self-actualization.

Consequently, married women of the fifties were perhaps more likely to view their tasks in the home as part of their proper occupation. Their career was traditionally defined in the wife, mother, and homemaker roles. Contemporary housewives, however, have now been sensitized to the controversies embedded in their roles. A greater freedom may now exist that encourages and supports housewives in their denouncement of the duties and tasks they perform in the home. Across time comparisons of the opinions full-time housewives have toward their work will now be used to determine whether such attitudinal shifts have occurred.

Opinion of Housework

Hypothesis: *Contemporary housewives are more dissatisfied with their work than were their counterparts twenty years ago.*

The following item is used to compare the 1957 and 1976 perceptions of housewives:

> Different people feel differently about taking care of a home—I don't mean taking care of the children, but things like cooking and sewing and keeping house. Some women look on these as just a job to be done—other women really enjoy them. How do you feel about this?

Responses were coded according to the following outline:

1. unqualified or qualified liking (like housework all the time, most of the time, or like certain aspects—no dislike mentioned)
2. ambivalent (like certain aspects, dislike others) or neutral response (responses not made in terms of likes or dislikes)
3. qualified or unqualified dislike (dislike housework all the time, most of the time, or dislike certain aspects—no likes mentioned)

Table 3-1 shows the distribution of responses to the opinion of housework item. In 1957, 68 percent of the housewives expressed a

Table 3-1
Opinion of Housework, 1957 and 1976
(percent)

Opinion of Housework	1957 (n = 627)	1976 (n = 335)
Positive	68	50
Neutral or ambivalent	27	44
Negative	5	6
Total	100	100
x^2 probability		<.0001 ($x^2 = 32, df = 2$)

positive opinion; this percentage decreased to 50 percent in 1976. The percentage of those expressing neutral or ambivalent feelings rose from 27 percent in 1957 to 44 percent in 1976. The percentage of those stating negative feelings remained relatively unchanged. This table suggests that, while the percentage of those expressing positive feelings decreased, there has not been a widespread rejection of housework. Rather than harbor general feelings of dislike for house-work, the 1976 housewives appear to have mixed feelings. The actual day-to-day tasks in and of themselves may not be very rewarding, yet task completion does contribute to the overall welfare of the family. This contradiction may be at the base of these neutral and ambiva-lent feelings. Instead of being more dissatisfied with their work in 1976, housewives may be more confused or more realistic about it.

Even though the percentage of those stating neutral or ambiva-lent feelings rose in 1976, it should not be overlooked that, for both years, the majority of housewives offer positive responses. This is interesting in light of the current assessments being made of house-work. Perhaps this suggests that the view of housework as dull, menial, isolating, and humiliating offered by some researchers and proponents of the women's movement is an orientation that is not espoused by the majority of people who are actually performing the work.

Because the central view inherent in this research is that changing times and the resulting ideological shifts are affecting individuals regardless of their structural positions, it is important to examine the relationship of selected demographic variables to housewives' opinion of housework. Table 3-2 offers the correlation of age of youngest child, education, and family income with opinion of housework. Because age and age of youngest child are highly correlated, age of youngest child are highly correlated, age of youngest child will be primarily used. Although both variables give information about one's position in the life cycle, the age of youngest child has perhaps more relevance for the family life cycle position of married women.

For 1957 and 1976, the older the youngest child, the more likely the mother is to express a positive opinion of housework. The direction of these rather weak correlations is not surprising if it is assumed that younger children generally add to the housework load. Younger children are probably more likely to soil, stain, spill, drop, dirty, and otherwise increase the amount of work to be done. Older children are probably more likely to reduce the work load by sharing

Table 3-2
Tau-Beta Correlations of Demographic Variables with
Opinion of Housework

Demographic Variables	Opinion of Housework	
	1957	*1976*
Age of youngest child	.132[a]	.105[a]
Education[b]	−.068[a]	−.214[a]
Family income	−.071[a]	−.029[a]

Note: Opinion of housework variable is categorized with three levels: (1) negative, (2) ambivalent or neutral, and (3) positive.
[a]Denotes statistical significance.
[b]The difference between the 1957 and 1976 *education* and *opinion of housework* correlations is statistically *significant*.

the housework responsibilities with the mother. It is little wonder then that mothers of older children are more likely to have a positive opinion of housework.

The relationship of education to opinion of housework changed significantly from 1957 to 1976. Whereas education is negatively related to housework opinions in both years, the 1976 relationship is much stronger than the 1957 one. Those individuals with higher levels of education may have goals and expectations that cannot be realized through the performance of household tasks. The achievement of a higher education may also reflect individual motivations and achievement orientation. These individuals may then be more dissatisfied with the work they are doing in the home. Oakley (1975) does maintain that housework cannot supply motivation or the means for self-actualization. Although this interpretation is applicable for postwar as well as contemporary housewives, education has emerged as a more powerful predictor of housework attitudes among the contemporary wives.

The relationship of family income to opinion of housework is negative and weak for either year, although the relationship is no longer statistically significant for 1976. Tsuchigane and Dodge (1974) note that—since World War II—decline in domestic workers, increase in suburbanization and home ownership, and devotion of more time to social activity have increased housework for higher-income wives.

As demographic shifts have occurred along the selected dimensions, bivariate relationships will now be utilized for specific across-time comparisons. It is important to determine whether the observed attitudinal change is a result of an ideological shift or the result of changes in the demographic redistribution of the population. Rather than being trichotomized, opinion of housework is now collapsed into a dichotomized variable reflecting "positive" versus "other" opinions of housework.

Table 3-3 looks at opinion of housework by age of youngest child. Whereas the 1976 mothers decreased at all levels in the percentage expressing positive opinions, the decreases for mothers with youngest child five years or under and mothers with youngest child 19 or over are statistically significant. If there has been an ideological shift discouraging positive feelings toward housework, the youngest mothers and the oldest ones appear to have been most affected.

The criticism of housework as being repetitious and never-ending

Table 3-3
Opinion of Housework by Age of Youngest Child, 1957 and 1976
(percent)

Youngest Child (years)	Opinion	1957	1976
0-5	Positive	61	40
	Other (neutral, ambivalent, negative)	39	60
	Total	100	100
	Number	265	102
	x^2 probability	<.001	
		$(x^2 - 12, df = 1)$	
6-12	Positive	62	49
	Other	38	51
	Total	100	100
	Number	106	79
	x^2 probability	not significant	
13-18	Positive	63	55
	Other	37	45
	Total	100	100
	Number	41	33
	x^2 probability	not significant	
19 and over	Positive	81	56
	Other	19	44
	Total	100	100
	Number	147	100
	x^2 probability	<.001	
		$(x^2 = 18)$	

may be very applicable to the mother of a preschool child (since the child probably adds to the work to be done). This mother, in 1976, is likely to be more aware of many of the less-than-positive sides of housework. Certainly she is less restrained in voicing her frustration, and the social climate is less repressive of these frustrations. The mother of older children in 1976 may be confronting the decreased importance of housework, especially if children are no longer in the home. Again, the social environment may have served to make her more aware and more expressive of negative feelings and attitudes.

Table 3-4 looks at opinion of housework by year and family income. In 1957, 77 percent of the low-income housewives had positive opinions of housework. By 1976, this percentage decreased to 52. Among the middle-income housewives, 65 percent in 1957 had positive housework opinions as compared to 50 percent in 1976. The figures for high-income wives are 66 percent and 48 percent, respectively. This table suggests that, at every income level, there have been significant decreases in the percentage of housewives expressing positive opinions of housework. For both years, low-

Table 3-4
Opinion of Housework by Family Income, 1957 and 1976
(percent)

Income Level	Opinion	1957	1976
Low	Positive	77	52
	Other (neutral, ambivalent, negative)	22	48
	Total	100	100
	Number	120	56
	x^2 probability	.001	
		$(x^2 = 12, df = 1)$	
Middle	Positive	65	50
	Other	35	50
	Total	100	100
	Number	309	111
	x^2 probability	$<.01$	
		$(x^2 = 8)$	
High	Positive	66	48
	Other	34	52
	Total	100	100
	Number	181	138
	x^2 probability	.001	
		$(x^2 = 11)$	

income housewives seem more likely to have positive opinions of housework. Yet, changes in opinions of housework do not appear to be particularly associated with any one income group.

Table 3-5 gives opinion of housework by year and education. For 1957, 72 percent of the less-than-high-school-educated, 65 percent of the high-school-educated, and 63 percent of the college-educated had positive opinions of housework. For 1976, the percentages are 68, 47, and 34, respectively. These findings reveal that the high-school-educated and those with college education have significantly altered their opinions of housework. Those with less than a high school education appear relatively unchanged on this question. The stronger association between education and housework opinions in 1976 is apparent. Whereas the college-educated are the least satisfied with housework in 1957 and 1976, the greatest 1957 to 1976 change has occurred among this group. This suggests that education may be a primary factor determining which individuals are more likely to be affected by changing norms and values.

The findings of table 3-5 raise an issue about the relationship between age, education, and opinion of housework. In 1957 and 1976, those with less than high school education may be found

Table 3-5
Opinion of Housework by Education, 1957 and 1976
(percent)

Education	Opinion	1957	1976
Less than high school	Positive	72	68
	Other (neutral, ambivalent, negative)	28	32
	Total	100	100
	Number	317	108
	χ^2 probability	not significant	
High school	Positive	65	47
	Other	35	53
	Total	100	100
	Number	212	134
	χ^2 probability	.001	
		$(\chi^2 = 11, df = 1)$	
College	Positive	63	34
	Other	37	66
	Total	100	100
	Number	95	92
	χ^2 probability	.0001	
		$(\chi^2 = 16)$	

among the older age groups. Hence, table 3-5 may be reflecting the bias related to age and not education. Table 3-6 looks at opinion of housework by age and education for 1957 and 1976. In 1957, it seems that housewives generally had positive views of housework. In 1976, however, regardless of age, the less-than-high-school-educated are more likely to have positive opinions of housework.

In reviewing the attitude change between the 1957 and 1976 respondents, the bivariate relationships indicate that the youngest and the oldest mothers, the high-school- and college-educated, and all income groups decreased significantly in the percentages reflecting positive opinions of housework.

Are More Housewives Planning to Work?

Hypothesis: *More contemporary housewives are planning to work in the future as compared with the postwar housewives.*

This hypothesis rests on the assumption that the current controversies attached to housework can serve as an impetus pushing house-

Table 3-6
Positive Opinion of Housework by Age and Education, 1957 and 1976

		Housewives Offering Positive Opinions			
		1957		*1976*	
Age (years)	*Education*	*Percent*	*Number*	*Percent*	*Number*
21-24	Less than high school	76	25	50	10
	High school	57	21	43	14
	College	66	9	43	7
25-34	Less than high school	55	67	75	16
	High school	64	93	39	38
	College	61	36	26	38
35-44	Less than high school	61	61	65	17
	High school	64	58	48	29
	College	54	26	37	16
45-54	Less than high school	79	66	62	21
	High school	76	25	48	29
	College	78	18	35	13
55 and over	Less than high school	84	98	73	44
	High school	67	15	58	24
	College	67	6	39	18

wives into the labor market. Work outside the home seems to now capture many of the positive features not associated with housework (for example, money, status, stimulation, social integration).

Housewives were asked the following question: Are you planning to work in the future? This item forms the basis of analysis in this section.

Table 3-7 looks at future plans by year. The figures indicate that, on an aggregate level, a significant increase has taken place in the percentage of housewives planning to work in the future. In 1957, 17 percent of the housewives planned to work in the future. By 1976, a total of 37 percent expressed these plans. (This increase is significant beyond the .0001 level.) Because of the demographic shifts that have also taken place, more detailed analysis is needed before the hypothesis can be validated.

Table 3-8 looks at the correlation of demographic variables with plans to work. Age here appears to be more relevant than does age of youngest child. What one plans to do in the future may be contingent on the amount of future available or remaining. Younger women have time to do a variety of things and engage in a variety of activities. An older woman may not have this type of perspective of her future. Instead of placing emphasis on the future, she may choose to be more reflective of her past. Indeed, the opportunities available to the older woman in the job market are rather limited. Hence, she may be very realistic in defining work out of her future.

In table 3-8, as can be expected, age is significantly related to plans to work in the future. Younger women are more likely to plan to work in the future. As can also be expected, higher education is positively related to plans to work in the future. Education does seem to set up goals and expectations that may not be met in the home. These results are applicable to both years. What is surprising is

Table 3-7
Housewives Who Plan to Work in Future, 1957 and 1976
(percent)

Plan to Work	1957 (n = 611)	1976 (n = 335)
Yes	17	37
No	83	63
Total	100	100
χ^2 probability	<.0001 ($\chi^2 = 49, df = 1$)	

Table 3-8
Tau-Beta Correlations of Demographic Variables with Plan
to Work in Future

	Plan to Work in Future	
Demographic Variables	1957	1976
Age[a]	$-.171^b$	$-.409^b$
Education[a]	$.042^b$	$.221^b$
Family income	$-.003$	$.003$

Note: Plan-to-work variable is dichotomized No-Yes.
[a]The difference between the 1957 and 1976 correlation of this variable with plan to work is statistically significant.
[b]Denotes statistical significance.

that family income is not significantly related to plans to work in the future. On an intuitive level, one would assume that family economic needs would be a force pushing housewives into the job market. Yet, for these 1957 and 1976 housewives, this is not the case. Perhaps those wives experiencing the greatest economic push to enter the labor market are already gainfully employed. It should not be overlooked that the relationships of age and education to future work plans have changed significantly from 1957 to 1976. These two demographic variables are much stronger predictors of the work plans for contemporary housewives than they were for the postwar wives.

Age and education become the central variables for 1957 and 1976 comparative purposes. Table 3-9 shows that, with the exception of the 55-and-over age group, all the age groups increased significantly in the percentage planning to work in the future. The largest increase occurs for those housewives in the 25-34 age range (from 19 percent in 1957 planning to work to 66 percent in 1976). This age group would include those women born during the "baby boom" years. These women may have deliberately postponed entry into the labor market to allow for concentration on childbearing and childrearing.

Table 3-10 focuses on plans to work by education and year. Each educational level has increased in the percentage planning to work in the future. The largest increase occurs for the college level (from 21 percent in 1957 to 53 percent in 1976). Education emerges again as having a significant impact on attitudes. The findings in table 3-10

Table 3-9

Housewives Who Plan to Work in Future by Age, 1957 and 1976
(percent)

Age (years)	Plan to Work	1957	1976
21-24	Yes	32	55
	No	68	45
	Total	100	100
	Number	54	31
	x^2 probability	$<.05$	
		$(x^2 = 4, df = 1)$	
25-34	Yes	19	66
	No	81	34
	Total	100	100
	Number	191	92
	x^2 probability	$<.001$	
		$(x^2 = 62)$	
35-44	Yes	23	39
	No	77	61
	Total	100	100
	Number	142	62
	x^2 probability	$<.05$	
		$(x^2 = 5)$	
45-54	Yes	11	26
	No	89	74
	Total	100	100
	Number	105	62
	x^2 probability	$<.01$	
		$(x^2 = 6)$	
55 and over	Yes	3	7
	No	97	93
	Total	100	100
	Number	119	88
	x^2 probability	not significant	

could also be tapping the effects of age. In 1957 and 1976, those persons with less than high school education may be found among the older groups. For this reason, it becomes necessary to look at the relationship between education and future work plans while controlling the respondent's age. Table 3-11 shows this relationship. Many of the numerical bases for percentages are too small to warrant discussion. Yet, some trends can be noted. Regardless of age, the less-than-high-school-educated housewives are the least likely to be planning to work in the future. In addition, the largest across-time increases in those planning to work are usually present among the

Table 3-10
Housewives Who Plan to Work in Future by Education, 1957 and 1976
(percent)

Education	Plan to Work	1957	1976
Less than	Yes	16	24
high school	No	84	76
	Total	100	100
	Number	310	109
	x^2 probability	.05	
		$(x^2 = 5, df = 1)$	
High school	Yes	17	37
	No	83	63
	Total	100	100
	Number	204	133
	x^2 probability	<.0001	
		$(x^2 = 18)$	
College	Yes	21	53
	No	79	47
	Total	100	100
	Number	94	92
	x^2 probability	<.0001	
		$(x^2 = 20)$	

college-educated wives. Thus, while controlling for age, the effects of education are still observable.

Although a trend may be taking place that sees more housewives entertaining future work plans, findings here would indicate that this trend has yet to gain widespread endorsement. The majority of housewives apparently still plan to continue in their housewife role. Shifts in the future work orientation of housewives do not seem to be occurring throughout the population. This is an attitudinal shift that appears to be related to the wife's structural location in the society. Younger housewives with higher levels of education stand out as those women likely to have plans to work in the future.

With the current emphasis on work as a means of achieving self-esteem and self-actualization, it seems reasonable to expect that the major reasons offered for future work plans in the seventies would differ from those offered in the fifties. More specifically, contemporary housewives planning to work may be more likely to offer noneconomic motives than were the postwar housewives.

For those housewives who had plans to work in the future a follow-up question was asked: "Women have different reasons for

Table 3-11

Housewives Who Plan to Work by Age and Education, 1957 and 1976

| | | Housewives Who Plan to Work | | | |
| | | 1957 | | 1976 | |
Age (years)	Education	Percent	Number	Percent	Number
21-24	Less than high school	48	25	70	10
	High school	20	20	43	14
	College	11	9	57	7
25-34	Less than high school	21	66	56	16
	High school	16	90	66	38
	College	23	35	71	38
35-44	Less than high school	18	61	23	17
	High school	23	55	31	29
	College	35	26	69	16
45-54	Less than high school	13	61	24	21
	High school	8	25	25	28
	College	11	18	31	13
55 and over	Less than high school	3	9	2	45
	High school	7	14	8	24
	College		6	17	18

working; what would be your main reason for working?" Responses were coded along the following dimensions:

1. economic factor (money)
2. positive ego satisfactions (such as feeling of accomplishment, independence, usefulness, etc.)
3. work as proper (it is the right thing to do)
4. prevents negative state (fills empty time, keeps one busy, etc.)
5. other reasons

Table 3-12 suggests that the distributions of 1957 and 1976 responses to this question do not differ significantly. Whereas the percentage of those giving economic reasons dropped in 1976 and the percentages giving ego-related reasons rose for that same year, these shifts in responses are not statistically significant. The majority of housewives in both years who plan to work offer economic reasons. Glenn (1959) and Sweet (1973) found similar results. Hence, a major change in the housewives' future motivation to work apparently has not occurred. Regardless of the nonmonetary value

Table 3-12
Reasons for Planning to Work, 1957 and 1976
(percent)

Reason	1957 (n = 103)	1976 (n = 124)
Economic motivation	59	49
Ego satisfaction	19	29
Work as proper	—	2
Prevents negative state	19	19
Other	3	1
Total	100	100
x^2 probability	not significant	

that seems currently attached to work outside the home, contemporary wives pinpoint economic incentives for future work plans as did the housewives of twenty years ago.

Conclusions

More contemporary housewives are expressing neutral or ambivalent feelings about housework, whereas postwar housewives generally had positive feelings about the work they did in the home. Because the current social climate maintains a more critical view of housework, attitudes of today's housewives are reflective of the controversy surrounding their activities as homemakers.

Whereas a significant increase was observed from 1957 to 1976 in the percentage of housewives who plan to work, the majority of housewives in both years do not plan to work in the future. In addition, economic reasons continue to be the most frequently cited motives for planning to work. The findings for 1976 are perhaps a bit more intriguing because of the less traditional orientation associated with the seventies.

In analyzing the plight of the modern housewife, several researchers have commented on the implications of this low-status work. Kreps (1972, p. 227) notes that, on the current scene, one of the most frequently cited complaints of women is the fact that they are expected to do routine, repetitive household chores for which there is no monetary reward. She adds that women are frequently eager to trade this work for a market job that pays a salary. Burke and Weir (1976, p. 285) imply that some wives may see employment as providing opportunities for accomplishment and creativity that are not found in the home; for feeling useful and competent with respect to the larger social milieu. Ferree (1975, p. 440) notes that, to keep anyone at home raising children and performing other life support functions, pay for housework might become necessary.

The findings in this chapter do not offer major support for these observations for the contemporary housewives. Wives who are full-time in the home are not planning a mass exodus to the labor market. A plausible explanation may rest in Oakley's distinction (1974) between doing housework and being a housewife. Whereas more wives feel ambivalent about their work, they still seem to be fairly satisfied with their housewife role. They can acknowledge dissatisfaction with the work and give more priority to the roles of wife and mother. Hence, doing housework is obviously only one part of a multifaceted role. Because the majority of 1976 housewives do not appear to be contemplating abandonment of their full-time housewife status, they may be very satisfied with being housewives.

In their study of the happiness and life satisfaction of wives who were "home market workers" and "labor market workers," Orden and Bradburn (1969) observed that housewives were indeed satisfied with their role. This suggests that housewives entertain certain commitments and responsibilities that are as meaningful to them as the employment commitment is for women who choose the labor market (Orden and Bradburn 1969, p. 402).

The bulk of the analysis in this chapter treated opinion of housework and future work plans as two separate variables. As the housewife's view of her work may influence her labor market plans, the relationship between these two variables is worthy of attention.

Table 3-13 looks at plans to work by housework opinions and year. In 1957, opinion of housework does not appear to be

Table 3-13
Housewives Who Plan to Work by Opinion of Housework, 1957 and 1976

	Housewives Who Plan to Work			
	1957		1976	
Opinion of Housework	Percent	Number	Percent	Number
Positive	15	419	28	167
Neutral, ambivalent	22	160	46	146
Negative	16	32	48	21

particularly related to plans to work. Of those housewives with positive opinions of housework, 15 percent plan to work in the future. For those with negative opinions, 16 percent plan to work in the future. The largest percentage of those planning to work comes from housewives with neutral or ambivalent opinions. During the postwar period, housewives' feelings toward their work was a nonissue. As a nonissue, there was really no reason for opinions of housework to be associated with or related to anything the wife did in the future. By 1976 this is no longer the case. Opinion of housework is related to future work plans. Those with neutral, ambivalent, or negative attitudes toward housework are more likely to be planning to work.

Several interpretations of these data are plausible. In 1958, Weiss and Samelson wrote that married women will only infrequently be motivated to seek careers because of the emptiness of housework. For the 1957 housewives, this position may be accurate. Although the data in table 3-13 do not make a case for causality, the 1976 results will challenge this observation. Housewives who view housework in neutral, ambivalent, or negative terms are more likely to be planning to work than those who hold positive opinions. While the majority of housewives are still not planning to trade their apron strings for a paycheck, the observed figures could indicate that this may no longer be the case over the next few years. The across-time results can easily be a reflection of a change that is taking place.

One final comment is necessary. In looking at changes in housewives' perceptions of their work, this discussion assumes that the nature of that work has remained fairly constant over time. This, of course, is not the case. Vanek (1974, p. 117) reviews the ways in which housework has changed. Less time is spent preparing food and cleaning up after meals. Laundry tasks have lightened because of detergents, automatic appliances, and wash-and-wear fabrics. A 1951 poll found that housewives disliked laundry and ironing the most when considering their housework chores (Gallup 1972). Hence, technological changes have served to lessen the wife's work in these areas. More time is now spent shopping, household managing, and traveling (to and from stores). Technological advancements and modernized kitchen gadgetry serve to reduce some of the pain and strain of housework while housework time has remained relatively unaffected. These changes should encourage housewives to have more positive views of their work. In spite of these housework improvements, fewer housewives actually hold positive opinions of their work.

4

Role Performance, Self-Perceptions, and Life Happiness: Does Work Make a Difference?

Wives and Employment: The "Added Burden" View

In 1959, Nolan and Tuttle wrote that the homemaker who under-took outside employment had to face the reality of assuming the major responsibility for two jobs—homemaking plus the paid job—and the possibility of community criticism. In 1976, Kreps and Leaper observed that, for the married woman, the paid job represents an additional occupation, which, when combined with home work, means that she is pursuing a "dual" career.

Because of the dual career activities of the employed wife, she may have an outlook on marriage and children different from her counterpart who is in the home full-time. This difference in outlook is expected to be more apparent in the fifties than in the seventies. The rationale here is that, during the postwar years, wives' awareness of the problems involved with combining the worker and wife roles was heightened by the prevailing social climate that endorsed the work-versus-home conflict perspective. Because these wives were being reminded of the conflicting obligations inherent in wife-work role integration, they were perhaps more aware of the demands associated with the wife and parent roles. Hence, these women were perhaps more likely than housewives to view the spouse and parent roles as constraining.

The presumably more supportive social environment of the seventies could imply that the worker-wife role combination is no longer perceived in critical terms. Formal and informal sources of support (friends, relatives, neighbors, Women's Liberation Movement, mass media, child-care facilities, for example) may have minimized concern over the conflicting obligations associated with the home-versus-job perspective. Since the social mandate placing wives "in the home" also appears to have eased somewhat, contemporary working wives may not be more likely than housewives to view marriage and children as constraints. Hence, differences in the

59

perceptions of the spouse and parent roles are not expected to be present between contemporary employed and nonemployed wives.

The 1957 working wife was also confronting issues related to adequate role performance. Operating norms dictated that the home was the primary focus for wives, and employment activities interfered with this focus. An implicit assumption was that the wife could not adequately perform her spouse, homemaker, and/or mother roles if she devoted time to labor-market participation. In such a nonsupportive social system, employed wives may have experienced guilt feelings over the performance of their home duties. The 1976 full-time homemaker should be relatively free from this anxiety. By 1976, concerns over role adequacy may have lessened for the employed wife, and she is not expected to differ from the housewife in her perceptions of role performance.

One's roles, one's level of competence in them, and one's feelings about them are an integral part of the self (Nye 1974, p. 207). The prevailing issues questioning the role performance of employed wives in 1957 would suggest that the self-concept and life happiness of the working wife would differ from that of the housewife. Feelings of guilt, anxiety, and role strain compounded by nonsupportive norms and cultural beliefs probably contributed to low self-esteem on the part of the working wife. Certainly the review of literature on housework presented earlier indicates that the home was perceived as the wife's natural place. In addition, the social climate of the postwar period defined a wife's occupation in terms of the homemaker role. Hence, the self-concept and general life happiness of the housewife is postulated to be higher than that of the employed wife. The working wife appeared to lack the formal and informal resources needed to support the integration of the homemaker-worker roles.

In the seventies, this situation is expected to be reversed. Whereas the postwar housewife was "in step" with the existing norms, the contemporary housewife is being bombarded with the exploitation of her role and the realization that her role may be "keeping her down." The work role has now been identified as a possible avenue to self-growth and social integration. Consequently, the favored position of the working wife is expected to be reflected in her higher self-concept and life happiness as compared to the nonworking wife.

A competing position would argue that, in both 1957 and 1976, the self-esteem of the employed wife is higher than that of the housewife. Ferree (1975) sees paid employment as possibly providing some relief from the problems of meaninglessness, powerlessness, and social isolation associated with housework. In her sample of working-class wives, she found that the working woman was happier than the housewife. She traced the satisfaction felt with work to the self-esteem it promoted. Komarovsky (1967) also maintains that pay for work carries with it a type of independence that enhances self-esteem. Burke and Weir (1976, p. 208) review studies revealing that working wives have higher self-esteem than nonworking wives. Chafe (1972, p. 220) suggests that gainful employment can provide women with a sense of personal and social worth that they may not find elsewhere. This position sees work outside the home as freeing women from the drudgery of housework. Working wives are able to engage in meaningful activities as a way of enhancing their self-esteem and becoming a part of the larger social structure. Feelings of self are also enhanced, because work for pay is valued. Through participation in this activity, a wife's self-concept would appear to be elevated. This view, however, is rejected here, because the notion that work for pay can lead to a wife's self-actualization seems to be a product of contemporary times and does not appear particularly relevant to the circumstances surrounding the postwar wife.

The following analysis attempts to test the across-time impact of employment on the role perceptions, role performance, self-perceptions, and life happiness of married women.

Role Perceptions and Role Performance

Hypothesis 1: *During the postwar years, working wives were more likely than housewives to see marriage and children as constraints. By 1976, this difference in role perceptions no longer exists.*

Wives were asked these questions: "First, thinking about a woman's life, how is a woman's life changed by being married? How is a woman's life changed by having children?" Responses to both questions were coded along a general outline that could be condensed into positive, ambivalent, neutral, or negative changes. Examples of responses for marriage and children are:

Changes	Marriage	Children
Positive	Someone to love	They make you happy
	Makes you happy	You feel loved
	Economic security	You feel important
Neutral, ambivalent	Have to get along	Life is different
	Makes you different	You're busier
	Settles you down	More responsibility
Negative	Someone bosses you	Tie you down
	Less freedom	More problems
	More cares, worries	

The responses were then recoded to determine whether respondents saw marriage or children as restricting, burdensome, or demanding. More than one response could be offered by respondents. All the responses offered by an individual were used for this recoding. Respondent's first mentioned reply, however, to how marriage and children change a woman's life is used for analysis of attitudes toward marriage and children.

Table 4-1 shows that working wives and housewives do not differ significantly in their attitudes toward marriage in either year. Thus, the hypothesized difference between the 1957 working and nonworking wives is not supported. Work status does not appear to be related to wives' perceptions of marriage. Although the work and wife roles were generally seen as incompatible in the postwar period, working wives do not appear to locate the source of this incompatibility within the institution of marriage. Socialization processes may dictate that attitudes related to marriage are developed well in advance of any labor-market behavior. If this is the case, then work activity would have little potential for influencing attitudes toward marriage. Slight period effects, however, are observable. By 1976, all wives have increased in the percentage expressing ambivalent or neutral marital attitudes. A less traditionally oriented society may witness more questioning of sex-role norms and stereotypes. Rather than being related to work status, changes in wives' perceptions of marriage appear to be associated with changing times.

Table 4-2 concentrates on wives' perceptions of children. Work status is not significantly related to wives' attitudes toward children

Table 4-1
Attitude toward Marriage by Work Status, 1957 and 1976
(percent)

	1957		1976	
	House-wives	Working Wives	House-wives	Working Wives
Attitude toward marriage				
Positive	39	35	28	30
Ambivalent or neutral	36	45	51	52
Negative	24	20	21	18
Total	100	100	100	100
Number	617	148	322	226
χ^2 probability	not significant		not significant	
Responses given that indicate marriage is restricting				
No responses	18	19	15	17
Some responses	35	30	30	30
All responses	47	51	55	53
Total	100	100	100	100
Number	616	147	322	225
χ^2 probability	not significant		not significant	

in either year. Working wives are slightly more likely to have positive views (60 percent) of the ways in which children change a woman's life than are housewives (51 percent) in 1957, but this difference is not significant. Significant differences, however, are found in the responses seeing children as restricting in 1957. Housewives were more likely to give some or all responses indicating that children were restricting, burdensome, or demanding (70 percent) as compared to working wives (58 percent). Perhaps these housewives were feeling tied down because of their children. Obviously working wives did not perceive children in this manner. Labor-force participation could be construed as a freedom from children not experienced by wives who are in the home full-time.

In 1976, attitudinal differences have disappeared between working and nonworking wives. Period effects do, however, seem to emerge. By the seventies, all wives have decreased in the percentage viewing children in a positive, nonrestrictive manner. Again, a less traditionally oriented society may see more wives raising questions (either because of a greater awareness or because of a greater freedom to vocalize) concerning the demands, responsibilities, and/or restrictiveness of the parental role.

Table 4-2
Attitude toward Children by Work Status, 1957 and 1976
(percent)

	1957		1976	
	House-wives	Working Wives	House-wives	Working Wives
Attitude toward children				
Positive	51	60	40	38
Ambivalent or neutral	26	25	34	39
Negative	23	15	26	23
Total	100	100	100	100
Number	618	141	329	230
x^2 probability	not significant		not significant	
Responses given that indicate children are restricting				
No responses	30	42	20	16
Some responses	38	33	36	39
All responses	32	25	44	45
Total	100	100	100	100
Number	614	141	329	228
x^2 probability	<.05 $(x^2 = 7, df = 2)$		not significant	

Consequently, more contemporary wives, regardless of work status, are expressing negative or ambivalent attitudes toward marriage and children. Certainly these wives are living in a social environment that makes them more cognizant of the limitations and liabilities inherent in the feminine role. Traditional norms may now be identified as the enemy of liberated women. This awareness of the oppressive aspects of traditional sex-role norms may result in more questioning of the rightful place of marriage and children in a woman's life. Many wives may be caught in the throes of sex-role controversy and perhaps even sex-role transition. Wives may now have legitimate reasons for feeling ambivalent and/or negative toward the traditional roles of spouse and parent.

General questions about the changes in a woman's life because of marriage and children tap a rather abstract level that may offer little insight into individual behavior. Responses may be removed from one's specific life situation. These questions are not very threatening and simply require that respondents be able to articulate their particular viewpoint. Because they do represent abstractions, these questions are not enough to provide information on the relationship between work status and role performance. To get at this relationship, these questions are analyzed: "Many women feel they're not as good (wives/mothers) as they would like to be. Have you ever felt this way? (If yes) What kinds of things have made you feel this way? Do you feel this way a lot of times, or only once in a while?" These questions will be used to test an assumption that role performance differences exist between working and nonworking wives of the postwar period.

Hypothesis 2: *In the postwar years, working wives were more likely to feel inadequate as a spouse and/or parent than housewives. By 1976, these differences do not exist.*

Table 4-3 shows no significant differences in perceptions of role adequacy among the wives for either year. Work status emerges as unrelated to general feelings of parental or spouse role performance. In 1957, for instance, 56 percent of the housewives as compared to 65 percent of the working wives had feelings of parental inadequacy. For the same year, 61 percent of the housewives versus 60 percent of the working wives had feelings of inadequacy as a spouse. The hypothesized difference in role performance between employed and nonemployed wives of 1957 is not supported.

Table 4-3
Feelings of Inadequacy as Parent by Work Status, 1957 and 1976
(percent)

	1957		1976	
	House-wives	*Working Wives*	*House-wives*	*Working Wives*
Ever felt inadequate				
as parent				
Yes	56	65	62	70
No	44	35	38	30
Total	100	100	100	100
Number	361	54	316	177
χ^2 probability	not significant		not significant	
Ever felt inadequate				
as spouse				
Yes	61	60	57	62
No	39	40	43	38
Total	100	100	100	100
Number	625	148	334	231
χ^2 probability	not significant		not significant	

Through her labor-force activity, a wife may feel that she is fulfilling her family obligations. Her income aids in the maintenance of her family. By helping to pay for a house, a car, or a child's future education, the employed wife's tangible contributions may offset any feelings of role inadequacy associated with the interference of work.

Although work status does not differentiate the feelings of role inadequacy among wives, it was anticipated that work status would shape the reasons offered for these feelings of inadequacy. Respondents were free to answer the open-ended follow-up questions in any manner they chose. Reasons for feelings of inadequacy as a spouse were coded along the following dimension.

1. role functioning (such as poor provider, poor housekeeper, compulsive housekeeper)
2. personal traits or vices (such as not kind enough, too bossy, not dependable)
3. other respondent characteristics (such as not healthy, mental problem)

Reasons for feelings of inadequacy as a parent were coded in the following general categories:

1. physical care, nurturing function not met
2. interpersonal relationship not adequate
3. disciplining function not adequately met
4. moral training function not adequately met
5. other teaching function not met
6. general (such as "lots of things")

Nolan and Tuttle (1958) found that employed wives cited "too little time for family" and "housework" as major disadvantages to working outside the home. Burke and Weir (1976) reported that "not having enough time to spend with family or for relaxation" to be one of the greatest concerns of working wives. Thus, it was expected that the 1957 working wives would offer "not enough time with children" and "poor, inadequate housekeeper" more often as reasons for feelings of role inadequacy than would housewives. This expectation is based on the assumption that, in a more traditionally oriented society, work was seen as competing with the home for the wife's time and energy. By 1976, these differences in the reasons underlying role inadequacy are not expected to be present.

Table 4-4 reveals that more 1957 working wives (24 percent) do cite not enough time with children than housewives (11 percent) as the basis for feelings of parental inadequacy. A surprising finding is that these differences persist in 1976. Ideological shifts that have taken place to incorporate work into the wife role have not liberated some working mothers from feeling that they should be spending more time with their children. In 1957 and 1976, working wives and housewives do not differ significantly in their citing of inadequate housekeeping as reason for feelings of spouse inadequacy, as also reflected in table 4-4. The working wife may simply be spending more weekend and evening time cleaning the house, and others in the household may be sharing in the housekeeping responsibilities. Keeping house then does not appear to be more of a problem for the wife who is participating in the labor force.

In 1957, the cultural mood of the day visualized work as interfering with the woman's place in the home. Home activities were seen as requiring full-time attention and the wife who was engaged in

Table 4-4

Reasons for Feelings of Inadequacy by Work Status, 1957 and 1976
(percent)

	1957		1976	
Reasons for Feelings of Inadequacy	*House-wives*	*Working Wives*	*House-wives*	*Working Wives*
As a parent				
Not enough time with children	11	24	15	27
Other	89	76	85	73
Total	100	100	100	100
Number	201	34	193	124
x^2 probability	.05		.01	
	$(x^2 = 4, df = 1)$		$(x^2 = 6, df = 1)$	
As a spouse				
Poor, inadequate housekeeper, inefficiency in the home	35	40	31	35
Other	65	60	69	65
Total	100	100	100	100
Number	371	82	178	139
x^2 probability	not significant		not significant	

labor-force activities was thought to be neglecting her home duties. To devote full time to work outside the home, something inside was obviously not being done. For this reason, it is expected that, twenty years ago, working wives had more frequent feelings of role inadequacy as compared to the housewife. For the 1976 working wives, however, a more relaxed social climate should alleviate some of these feelings of role inadequacy. By 1976, the housewives and working wives should not differ in the frequency of feelings of role inadequacy.

Table 4-5 shows that working mothers in 1957 were more likely to have frequent (a lot, often) feelings of parental inadequacy (53 percent) as compared to housewives (31 percent). In 1976, no significant differences emerge. Employed mothers have decreased sharply in the percentage having frequent feelings of not doing a good job as a mother (29 percent) and are at the same level as housewives (29 percent). Frequency of feelings related to spouse inadequacy, on the other hand, do not differ significantly by work status for either year.

The findings for role perception and role performance reveal that, for working wives, the parental role has been one of paramount concern. The combining of the worker-wife roles does not appear to interfere with housekeeping duties in 1957 and 1976. Yet persons

Table 4-5
Frequency of Feelings of Inadequacy by Work Status, 1957 and 1976
(percent)

Frequency of Feelings of Inadequacy	1957		1976	
	House-wives	Working Wives	House-wives	Working Wives
As a parent				
A lot, often	31	53	29	29
Once in a while	69	47	71	71
Total	100	100	100	100
Number	193	34	193	121
χ^2 probability	.01 $(\chi^2 = 6, df = 1)$		not significant	
As a spouse				
A lot, often	20	26	21	20
Once in a while	80	74	79	80
Total	100	100	100	100
Number	358	82	183	141
χ^2 probability	not significant		not significant	

who combined the wife-mother-worker roles did experience frequent feelings of parental inadequacy in 1957 and were somewhat more likely to feel they were not spending enough time with their children in both 1957 and 1976.

It seems obvious that the problem of juggling three roles are more numerous than the problems of integrating two roles. Issues of work strain and role overload surface to highlight the unique situation of the married working woman who is also a mother. Cultural mandates associated with motherhood are very pervasive and women appear to take this role very seriously (whether because of choice or socialization). Mothers do have valid concerns about the well-being of their children and may be anxious to provide whole-some environments for children in their absence. Responsibility for childrearing cannot be delayed until the weekends or evenings (like housework). By 1976, the working mother may not have more frequent feelings of parental inadequacy as compared to her counter-part in the home, but she does tend to worry a little more than the home mother about not spending enough time with her children.

As the activities of one's life and the existing social environment may have a tremendous potential for affecting one's perceptions of self, the impact of work status on wife's self-perceptions will now be investigated.

Work and Self-Perceptions

Hypothesis 1: *In the fifties, housewives were more likely to have positive self-perceptions than were working wives. By 1976, this situation has reversed.*

If one's role identification receives the approval and support of others, feelings of self-worth may be boosted. The effects of a changing social environment are expected to differentiate the self-perceptions of wives. This question is used to measure wives' self-perceptions: "People are the same in many ways, but no two people are exactly alike. What are some of the ways in which you are different from other people?" In analyzing this question, Gurin, Veroff, and Feld (1960) expected to determine the respondent's general picture of themselves. The neutral character of the question made it possible for strong or weak points to be mentioned. These investigators devised a rating scale that ran from very positive ("I'm a very competent person") to very negative ("I'm the kind of person who can't get along with people") with a midpoint of ambivalence, that is, a combination of positive and negative self-descriptions with neither orientation predominating (see Gurin, Veroff, and Feld 1960, p. 54). (The neutral midpoint was omitted from analysis here because of the difficulty of interpreting its meaning.)

Table 4-6 reports no significant differences in the self-perceptions of working wives and housewives for either year. In 1957, 66 percent of the housewives and 70 percent of the working wives maintained positive feelings about themselves. For 1976, the percentages are 74 and 77, respectively. In both years, working wives are somewhat more likely to have positive images of self than are the housewives. These differences are not sufficient enough to warrant major consideration. This lack of significant differences suggests that one's level of self-acceptance has little to do with a specific role one is occupying. Working or not working would indicate one aspect of life, whereas general self-perceptions would take into account life in its totality. In forming self-images individuals can draw on their strengths from a number of possible areas.

It should not be overlooked that the majority of wives in each year have positive feelings about themselves. The 1976 percentages show a slight increase among those with positive perceptions. Regardless of the controversy going on concerning women's roles, most wives are maintaining positive images of themselves.

Whereas work status does not differentiate the self-related attitudes of wives in general, this work status may hold numerous unique implications for mothers. These implications are captured in Hypothesis 2.

Table 4-6
Wives' Self-Perceptions by Work Status, 1957 and 1976
(percent)

	1957		1976	
	House-wives	*Working Wives*	*House-wives*	*Working Wives*
Self-Perceptions	*(n = 447)*	*(n = 99)*	*(n = 225)*	*(n = 175)*
Positive	66	70	74	77
Ambivalent	15	17	9	11
Negative	19	13	16	12
Total	100	100	100	100
χ^2 probability	not significant		not significant	

Hypothesis 2: *In the fifties, working mothers' self-perceptions were lower than those of home mothers. In addition, the working mothers' self-perceptions were related to the age of their youngest child. By 1976, these differences are no longer visible.*

In 1957, the mother's place was rigidly confined to the home, especially if she had a young child. Structural limitations almost demanded that mothers of preschoolers be the primary caretakers for their children. Day-care centers were scarce, and the mother who sought outside employment may have been confronted with child-care problems. The working mother was probably more likely to feel "just awful" about herself—because norms dictated that she should and because the need for adequate child supervision was a pressing concern. As younger children may also require more care and attention than older ones, working mothers with a younger child may have been particularly likely to feel guilty about "abandoning" their child. As the social norms ease, working mothers may be more liberated from traditional sex-role expectations.

Table 4-7 compares the self-perception responses of working mothers and home mothers by year and age of youngest child. This table allows for within-year and across-year comparisons. In 1957, home mothers with preschool-aged youngest child were more likely to hold positive views of themselves (62 percent) than were the working mothers (42 percent). The difference between these two groups of mothers is significant. Home mothers and working mothers with youngest child falling in the older age categories do not differ significantly in their self-perceptions. Another finding surfaces from the 1957 figures: as the age of youngest child increases, working mothers' self-perceptions become more positive. For the mothers working in a more traditional time period, 42 percent with a preschool-aged child, 68 percent with a grade-school-aged child, 86 percent with a high-school-aged child, and 90 percent with a youngest child 19 or older hold positive opinions of themselves. Such a linear trend is not found among the home mothers.

In 1976, home mothers and working mothers do not differ significantly in their self-perceptions regardless of the age of their youngest child. The linear relationship between positive self-perceptions and age of youngest child no longer exists for the contemporary working mothers. The majority of all mothers in each youngest child age group maintain positive self-perceptions.

No significant across-year changes emerge for the mothers who

Table 4-7

Self-Perceptions of Mothers by Work Status and Age of Youngest Child, 1957 and 1976

(percent)

Age of Youngest Child (years)	Self-Perceptions	1957		1976	
		Home Mothers	Working Mothers	Home Mothers	Working Mothers
0-5	Positive	62	42	73	75
	Ambivalent	17	50	7	12
	Negative	21	8	20	13
	Total	100	100	100	100
	Number	192	12	73	32
	x^2 probability	<.05		not significant	
6-12	Positive	70	68	70	78
	Ambivalent	11	21	14	7
	Negative	19	11	16	15
	Total	100	100	100	100
	Number	73	28	57	46
	x^2 probability	not significant		not significant	
13-18	Positive	63	86	74	65
	Ambivalent	17	7	16	13
	Negative	20	7	10	22
	Total	100	100	100	100
	Number	30	14	19	23
	x^2 probability	not significant		not significant	
19 or over	Positive	73	90	84	88
	Ambivalent	15	5	5	3
	Negative	11	5	11	9
	Total	100	100	100	100
	Number	105	20	62	33
	x^2 probability	not significant		not significant	

were in the home on a full-time basis. For the working mothers, however, a significant change occurred for those with a youngest child under six. In 1957, 42 percent of these mothers had positive self-perceptions. By 1976, this percentage had increased to 75. This shift represents an increase that is significant beyond the .05 level. No other significant across-year shifts are observed among working mothers.

The working mother of 1976 with a preschool child may no longer be confronting numerous problematic issues around the place of work in her life. She may be freer to pursue her job in an environment that begins to recognize the legitimacy of day-care centers. Structural changes such as these could reflect a greater acceptance of the working mother who has a younger child. These findings do, however, raise questions about the role of norms in the shaping of individual level attitudes and self-perceptions.

The role of work status and changing times in shaping wives' perceptions of their current life happiness will now be explored.

Work and Life Happiness

Hypothesis 1: *In 1957, housewives were happier than working wives. By 1976, the situation has reversed, and working wives are now happier with their lives.*

The measure of general life happiness is based on the question: "Taking things all together, how would you say things are these days—would you say you're very happy, pretty happy, or not too happy these days?"

Table 4-8 shows that, in both 1957 and 1976, working wives are slightly happier than housewives, but these differences are only significant in 1976. In 1957, 44 percent of the housewives are "very happy" as compared to 50 percent of the working wives. In 1976, working wives have maintained this percentage, while housewives have decreased slightly in their level of happiness (40 percent are "very happy"). The table reveals that regardless of year and work status, wives are generally happy with their lives. The hypothesized differences based on changing social norms are not supported. In this

Table 4-8
Wives' Present Happiness by Work Status, 1957 and 1976
(percent)

Present Happiness	1957		1976	
	House-wives (n = 626)	Working Wives (n = 149)	House-wives (n = 334)	Working Wives (n = 229)
Very happy	44	50	40	50
Pretty happy	50	43	56	46
Not too happy	6	7	4	5
Total	100	100	100	100
χ^2 probability	not significant		<.05	
			$(\chi^2 = 7, df = 2)$	

analysis, work is powerless in distinguishing the life happiness of wives.

Conclusions

In studying the across-time attitudes of working and nonworking wives toward role orientation, role perceptions, self-perceptions, and life happiness, several findings are worthy of comment here. Whereas housewives and working wives in 1957 and 1976 do not differ in their attitudes toward the spouse role, 1957 housewives were more likely than working wives to view children in restricting, burdensome terms. In this same year, working mothers were more likely than housewives to have frequent feelings of parental inadequacy. By 1976, housewives and working wives do not differ either in their perceptions of children or in the frequency of their parental inadequacy feelings.

The 1957 role performance perceptions related to the parent role could suggest that the defined responsibilities associated with motherhood were more demanding than those associated with marriage. In addition, society was still more likely to define traditionally the place of the young child—by the side or in the arms of his or her mother. In the seventies, traditionalism appears to have been attacked. Period effects are apparent in the lower percentage of all wives who express positive attitudes toward children.

In 1957 and 1976, no differences are observed in the self-perceptions of working and nonworking wives. In looking at mothers, some differences do surface. During the postwar years, working mothers who had a youngest child five years old or younger were less likely to have positive perceptions of themselves as compared to nonworking mothers. Also, as the age of the youngest child increased, the working mother was also likely to increase in her positive self-perceptions. By 1976, these trends are no longer visible.

Assessment of life happiness does not differ significantly between working and nonworking wives in 1957. By 1976, working wives tend to be slightly happier than nonworking wives. Overall, a general finding is that the fact of wife's employment seems to have minimal importance in differentiating the attitudes wives have toward themselves, their roles, and their current assessment of life happiness.

5 Conclusions and Implications

Summary of Major Findings

Traditional sex-role norms have been affected by the conditions of social change. Some of these conditions include the rise in the labor-force participation of married women, the increase in labor-saving home products, trends reflecting smaller families, greater state responsibility for child-rearing, and a political movement concerned with women's equality. This research has focused on another indicator of social change—the across-time comparisons of married women's attitudes toward their work.

The 1957 study captured a period that was supportive of traditional sex role norms. This postwar era was reacting to the increase in the labor-force activity of wives brought on by the labor shortage of World War II. Manifestations of this reaction were seen in public attitudes disapproving of working wives and in the popular view that work served to masculinize women. Hence, women were encouraged to maintain their femininity by defining their place within the boundaries of the home. In the midst of this social climate, the labor-force participation of married women continued to rise. Because this participation could be defined as helping the family, apparently wives' labor-force activity could be tolerated. Economic incentives were usually cited as the primary factor motivating women to work.

The 1976 replication study captures a markedly different time period. Working wives have continued to increase their labor-force participation, but public opinion no longer frowns on this labor activity. Perhaps the passage of time and these rising rates mean that working wives cease to be oddities and begin to be an established part of American life.

The time intervening between 1957 and 1976 saw increased public awareness of the issues related to sex-role inequalities. Mass media carried the views of the Women's Liberation Movement protagonists and antagonists to American homes across the country.

75

Proponents of the Movement urged women to seek self-actualization in the labor market and to denounce their exploitation in the home as unpaid workers. In 1957, the role of homemaker appears to have been idealized, whereas the working wife had some degree of stigma attached to her. By 1976, a type of reversal has taken place. The housewife now needs to defend her role, whereas the working wife has gained more acceptance.

The across-time comparisons of wives' attitudes toward their work do indicate that attitudinal changes have taken place. For instance, a significant increase has occurred among those wives expressing a noneconomic commitment to work from 1957 to 1976. Regardless of age of the youngest child present in the home, wife's educational level, and family income, a dramatic increase is observed in the percentage of 1976 wives saying they would continue to work in the absence of financial need. Because this attitudinal change is so pervasive among all the contemporary working wives, an ideological shift has occurred that supports wives' working for reasons other than money.

Although the percentage of noneconomically committed wives rose from 58 percent in 1957 to 82 percent in 1976, it should not be overlooked that many working wives of the postwar period were attaching a nonmonetary value to work. Even during the time when they received a minimum of encouragement toward this type of commitment, some wives were, nonetheless, developing it. Wives' participation in the labor force has, however, usually been framed in a work-home conflict perspective. Because the study of wives' feelings of attachment to work and the meaningfulness of work in their lives was typically overlooked in the fifties, even in the sixties, it is apparent that social definitions served as a guide for the identification of research questions.

In 1957, those wives who did express a noneconomic work commitment saw work as a means of keeping busy and filling otherwise empty time. In 1976, more wives are citing the meaningfulness and usefulness of work as the basis of their noneconomic work commitment. These ego-satisfying reasons for working were generally offered by those wives with some college education.

In 1957, about a quarter of the employed wives wanted to be home full-time. By 1976, the percentage preferring full-time housework dropped to a negligible 3 percent. Labor-force participation has emerged as a choice for the working wives of the seventies—a choice that many postwar wives did not have.

Rather than favor full-time housework, more employed wives of 1976 prefer another kind of work. Their current work environment is obviously on some vital dimension. For one thing, contemporary female workers are more aware of sex segregation and sex inequalities in the marketplace than were their 1957 counterparts. Unfair recruiting, hiring, and promoting practices were just as much a part of the fifties as they are the seventies. The difference lies in the public's current identification of these issues as clear violations of women's rights. Sex discrimination is now recognized as a national social concern warranting governmental intervention.

Overall, work has taken on a broader, more significant meaning for working wives. Work is no longer just a money-making activity but an activity that provides satisfying and rewarding experiences.

Full-time housewives have also been affected by the changes occurring in society. In 1957, wives uniformly held positive opinions about their work in the home. The ideology of that period endorsed the housewife role so that persons in that role accepted the tasks associated with it. In 1976, however, a significant number of housewives have mixed feelings about their work in the home. They readily admit that they like performing some tasks and dislike doing others, or they simply see their activities as things that just have to be done. Contemporary housewives are more attuned to both the positive and negative sides of housework. This more realistic assessment of within the home chores is not observed among those housewives who did not complete high school. Regardless of age, the less-educated housewives expressed positive opinions about their work.

In 1976, wives are very much aware of the controversies surrounding the role of housewife. Housework, because of its unpaid status, is currently being referred to as exploitative by women's liberationists and feminists. Housewives have also been made more aware of the drudgery, meaninglessness, powerlessness, and emptiness of household chores. Consequently, the societal devaluation of housework and recognition of the generally menial nature of the tasks are factors contributing to the negative opinions given by the housewives in 1976. The less-educated contemporary housewives, however, are unaffected by these factors.

Whereas more wives in 1976 plan to work in the future than did in 1957, the majority of housewives in both years do not define work outside the home as part of their future. Those wives who are planning to work generally offer an economic reason as the primary motivating factor. In addition, the college-educated housewives of 1976 are usually the ones anticipating labor-force entry. Although more contemporary housewives have mixed feelings about housework, they are not planning to relinquish their housewife role. This indicates that household tasks are only one aspect of the role. Acceptance of the role does not preclude the questioning of some of the activities and behavior associated with that role.

This research also looked at the fact of employment to determine if observable differences existed among working and nonworking wives. Very few differences emerged, and those that did occurred among mothers in particular. In 1957, the working mother who had a preschool-aged child was more likely to have negative feelings about herself than was the nonworking mother. In 1976, this difference has also disappeared.

These differences among the 1957 working and nonworking mother can easily reflect the lack of formal and informal sources of support available to the working mother. Traditional sex-role norms were more strictly applied in her case, especially if she had a young child. She also had to confront the possibility that her working could have adverse effects on the child. Because the largest recent increase in labor-force participation has occurred for the mothers of preschoolers, these mothers are among the last to be liberated from the home. For the 1976 working mother, more supports are available. As the number of working mothers increases, the employed mother is less likely to be perceived as a social problem. The increase in the labor-force participation of mothers has been accompanied by an increase in child-care facilities. The presence of such facilities is instrumental in freeing the mother from worry about the supervision of the child in her absence.

For wives in general, the fact of employment makes no difference in self-perceptions and little difference in the assessment of overall life happiness. In 1957 and 1976, wives generally have positive feelings about themselves and tend to be happy with their lives. This result suggests that, as controversies surface over women's roles and as sex-role redefinitions occur, the majority of wives of 1976 are not experiencing noticeable adverse effects along the self-perception and life happiness dimensions studied here.

Consequently, results show that changing attitudes are associated with changing times. Causality was never hypothesized. It was not within the scope of this book to prove that the illustrative conditions of social change caused women to alter their attitudes. The current social environment is more supportive and tolerant of behavior and ideas that were once defined as deviant. Social issues emerged in the seventies that raised the public's awareness of the controversies associated with the female role. Regardless of causality theories, changing views among wives are accompanying the other changes occurring in society.

The positions of employed and nonemployed wives in America are far from ideal. The changes cited highlight stages of a process. More needs to be known about working wives and housewives as the transition from old norms to new continues. This generation of knowledge provides a sound base for interventive strategies that will make the process of change less problematic for wives and society in general.

Implications: Working Wives

Because contemporary working wives have more of a noneconomic commitment to work, more needs to be known about the attachment these women have to work. The measure of work commitment used in this study is very similar to the one employed by other researchers interested in this topic. Now that the increase in the noneconomic work commitment of wives has been documented, it is time to move beyond simplistic, unidimensional operationalizations to the development of more refined measures.

Several researchers have proposed methods for detailed investigations of labor-force attachment. Safilios-Rothschild (1971, p. 491) acknowledges that the conceptualization of work commitment as uninterrupted work participation—even when children are young and when financial needs do not dictate the married woman's gainful employment—is well suited to the particular case of married women. However, as these women increase in their labor-force participation, they may no longer need to be viewed as a special case. Indeed, this increase may minimize the differences existing among these women and other labor-force participants. For this reason, a more universal conceptualization of work commitment would be needed. Safilios-Rothschild suggests that a universal measure of work commitment applicable to both men and women could be based on the relative distribution of interest, time, energy, and emotional investment in work as compared with other life sectors.

Another researcher, Maret-Havens (1977), has developed an index to measure labor-force attachment among women. Her index ranges from career (continuous, year-round, and full-time employment) to none (no labor-force participation history) in types of attachment. This index emphasizes the place of job history in determining labor-force attachment; an uninterrupted record of full-time employment defines those with the strongest work attachment. Hence, whether wives are working at the time a survey is undertaken overlooks variations in work history. This variation may be crucial in identifying the work commitment characteristics of wives.

These observations indicate that there are many aspects to the work commitment of wives. Whereas work in the absence of financial need certainly gives insight into one aspect of this commitment, it is quite clear that this insight does not make up a total picture. Obviously, interested researchers must deal with the complexities of the issue by expanding the conceptualization related to labor-force attachment and by developing measures that can adequately tap this attachment.

In addition to research issues, policy issues surface. Policy implications cited here deal with three issues: sex discrimination in the marketplace, services needed by working wives, and the need for child-care facilities.

As more and more wives engage in gainful employment for reasons other than financial, they are becoming more aware of the unique problems they encounter as they participate in the labor force. As the work life of wives lengthens, wives may be more concerned about the meaningfulness of their work and their opportunities for advancement. Efforts may also be made to decrease the concentration of women in sex-typed occupations such as secretary-stenographer, bookkeeper, school teacher, and social worker.

A wider dispersion of women throughout the labor force could be supported and encouraged by a number of policies. Specific hiring requirements should be tailored to fit the job. Physical requirements that are used to delimit the number of women in a particular field may be unjustly used. In addition, technological innovations lessen the strength requirements in operative and other jobs (Hedges 1970, p. 20). This would suggest that more equitable hiring practices can be employed as a means of guaranteeing the equal access of women to a wider variety of jobs.

Hedges (1970, p. 19) notes that the limited kinds of jobs in which women are employed are, for the most, extensions of the work women have done in the home. Women were hired to perform such tasks as the care of the sick, the instruction of children, food preparation, cleaning and serving, and the paperwork for institutions and offices. As traditional sex-role norms decline in universal acceptance, it seems reasonable to expect that sex segregation on the job will also decline. Affirmative action strategies, antidiscrimination laws, and the issues raised by the Equal Rights Amendment suggest that this decline can be better increased by social policy than by being left as a chance occurrence.

The working wife also encounters a number of problematic situations away from the job. Darley (1976, p. 94) notes that women who combine a career with wifehood and motherhood may be confronted with an ambiguous situation because the standards are contradictory, that is, to be good in one role implies relative failure in another. These women have a work reference group and a family reference group, and the ranges of evaluations associated with each group vary considerably. Darley maintains that a third kind of reference group will emerge if the number of women combining these contradictory roles increases. Working wives could form their own meeting groups in an attempt to enhance their individual strengths, to encourage each other, and to provide needed social support. Employers as well as community agencies could facilitate the development of these groups.

Beckett (1976, p. 468) maintains that the average wife will probably be concerned about entering or reentering the labor force, about the attitude of her husband, the problems of adequate child care, and the effect that working has on her children. Beckett also identifies a number of services that can be provided by community agencies: skill development; therapy for individuals, couples, and families; job counseling; and knowledge of day-care facilities and other pertinent community resources. Hedges (1970, p. 29) points out the need for improvements in the counseling and occupational preparation for women. Kanter (1977, p. 96) echoes that attention should be given to community services that will provide aid and support to employed married women.

The plight of the working mother may be eased somewhat through greater availability of child-care facilities. Lack of adequate care for children of working mothers is not only a serious obstacle to the employment of women; it is a matter of social concern as to the welfare of the children (Hedges and Barnett 1972, p. 12). Whereas an increase is needed in community-based child-care facilities, Kanter (1977b) suggests that worksite day-care could be investigated as a feasible possibility.

Whereas working wives may be freer to develop attachments to the labor market, they are certainly not free from all the conflicts and ambiguities surrounding their integration of social roles. Much can be done to lessen the problems inherent in combining two major roles.

Implications: Housewives

This research revealed that housewives have changed their opinions about the work they do in the home. More wives are now expressing ambivalent feelings about this work. Additional research is needed to uncover the nature and sources of this disenchantment.

Housewives themselves do not form a homogeneous group. Hence it is important to pinpoint those dimensions along which they differ. These dimensions could also provide additional insight into their work-in-the-home attitudes. One such dimension could be the role of leisure activities in shaping the housewife's attitudes. Non-working wives are more likely than working wives to be involved in community organizations and to hold a position of leadership in these organizations (Nye 1963b, p. 368). This community activity could provide numerous social contacts and opportunities for civic involvement that is meaningful to housewives. Such activity may be useful in determining the ways in which housewives define their existence.

Much of the rhetoric against housework ignores many aspects of the housewife's role. These homeworkers are not confined to the home, destined for an existence of loneliness. There are opportunities for frequent contact with other housewives and participation in civic activities. These factors could be instrumental in determining whether a housewife is planning to work in the future. Those with days saturated with meaningful social activities may not be the ones planning to work as a means of escaping the "emptiness" and "loneliness" of the home. Housework typically has not been viewed as real work. Hence, little is known about those factors impinging on the work attitudes of housewives. As more attention is being focused on the social roles of women, this area will command more attention.

Another research area exists for housewives. The majority of housewives in 1957 and 1976 do not plan to work in the future. This result could reflect these women's choice or their sense of duty. Ferree (1975, p. 439) concluded that many working-class full-time housewives do not seek employment because of their feeling of lack of power to determine their own lives. These women were seen to believe more in duty than rights. Ferree does add that there is no reason to assume that no one could be a perfectly contented and self-actualizing adult in the homemaker role. Thus, it becomes crucial to identify the reasons many wives spend their present and plan to spend their future in the housewife role. If it is a sense of duty that compels them, then writers can continue to degrade the role of women in the home. If it is by choice that they are in the home, then a more realistic appraisal should be made of the social rewards contained in homemaking.

The role of housewife involves far more than cleaning, cooking, and sewing. Concentration on specific household tasks often serves to undermine the very nature of this social role. Enlightened, liberated researchers should consider all aspects of this role before making sweeping generalizations. Because the majority of housewives plan to continue in this role, it is not a "social disease" but rather a viable way of enhancing feelings of self-worth.

Because so many questions surround the role of the housewife, policy implications are difficult to formulate in the absence of relevant research. Several writers speak of the possible need to pay housewives for their home work (see Ferree 1975 and Kreps 1972). Whereas this research found that more contemporary wives have ambivalent feelings about housework, it is not known to what extent, if any, payment for housework would alter their views. Certainly more information is needed before social policy can seriously be contemplated in this area.

Whereas the shortage of child-care facilities has often been cited as a factor keeping mothers in the home, it is difficult to predict the effect of increased child-care facilities on the plans of housewives to work. Those mothers who work do appear to find some way of making arrangements for their children. It does seem reasonable that those mothers desiring to enter the labor market could also reach some resolution around child care. It is also quite reasonable to assume that many housewives have deliberately opted to devote their time and energy (full-time) to the care and nurturing of their families. Until more definitive research is undertaken, speculations and informed opinions will continue to predominate.

Implications: General Issues

The importance of education in shaping individual aspirations cannot be overlooked. Many of the changes observed in the attitudes of wives were associated with more educated women. This could suggest that, as the educational level of the general population continues to rise, more women will be espousing nontraditional views. This could also suggest that eventually these attitude changes will filter to the other educational levels. Kreps (1972, p. 232) makes an observation applicable to all women:

> It seems unlikely that American women, *particularly the college educated*, will again give home work and child care the central role they occupied in the 1940s and 1950s. (Emphasis added.)

This would suggest that a movement away from traditionalism is associated with educational attainment.

In 1964 Degler wrote that most American women were interested in jobs, not careers. As labor-force attachment increases with the lengthening of wives' work life and as the educational level of wives increases, it seems likely that more wives will develop career aspirations. Work commitment may eventually give way to career commitment.

Another shaper of individual level attitudes is race. Whereas this research used white wives only, a number of questions surface about the work attitudes of black wives. Their work history in America reveals patterns that are unlike those of white women. The forces affecting black employment differ from those associated with whites. Hence the work attitudes of black wives cannot be expected to parallel those of white wives. For this reason, many of the issues raised should be explored with minority wives.

Labor-force participation among wives and mothers has been a vital aspect of black family life. This participation is usually explained by researchers as a family adjustment to oppressive economic conditions. It is not known to what extent work commitment among black wives reflects an economic basis or a belief in the meaning and philosophy of work. Little is known about black wives' perceptions of the housewife role. Is this a role that most of them long for because they really do not want to work anyway? Is it an ideal choice they wish they could make? Is their work role forced upon them? Clearly, the data on majority wives cannot be extrapolated to the case of minority wives. Sources of social support, child-care facilities, role of husband, inequality in the workplace are relevant topics for these women also. Black women are further victimized if sweeping generalizations are made based on studies of white women.

A Concluding Remark

The 1957 and 1976 surveys captured two different snapshots of American life. Putting these two static snapshots together reveals a picture of the dynamic processes occurring over time. Social change is continuous. Certainly changes taking place around the role and status of American women are far from complete. A 1980 snapshot would no doubt produce even more indicators of social change.

The 1957 snapshot is intriguing. The postwar era witnessed a rise in fertility. A considerable part of this baby boom resulted from an increase in the proportion of women of childbearing age who had ever married and from the tendency of couples to have babies when economic conditions are favorable (see Kiser, Grabill, and Campbell 1968, pp. 113, 253). The normative structure was sympathetic to and supportive of this increased fertility, because traditional values gained a new momentum. The roles of wife and mother were defined, with fervor, to be the most important roles a woman could have. All these factors appear to have been forces keeping women out of the labor market. At the same time, the labor-force participation of wives was still rising. This rise has been attributed to the shortage of single women needed to meet the demands of the labor market (Oppenheimer 1970). Labor-force conditions were exerting pressures drawing wives into the labor market.

Hence, the fifties represents a unique interaction between demographic and social factors, because two countervailing trends were apparently operating. The inconsistency between these opposing trends may have been minimized by social standards "permitting" wives to work provided that they justified their work primarily on the basis of economic, helpmate motives.

The 1976 snapshot focuses on a much different period. Decreased fertility, increased economic stress, and the demands of the labor market are cited as contemporary forces impinging on wives' labor-market activity. All these forces encourage the labor-force participation of wives. At the same time, the current normative structure is more tolerant and even more supportive of working wives.

Structural changes have indeed taken place. Labor-force participation rates, size of families, and economic conditions are only examples of some of the areas in which social changes have occurred. This book proves that structural modifications are being accompanied by profound changes in the attitudes of wives.

Appendix A
Demographic
Distributions for
Wives, 1957 and 1976

Table A-1

Demographic Shifts Occurring Between 1957 and 1976,
Samples by Employment Status

(percent)

Characteristics	1957		1976	
	Home Wives	Labor Wives	Home Wives	Labor Wives
Age (years)				
21-24	9	5	9	13
25-34	31	29	27	36
35-44	23	31	18	20
45-54	18	27	19	21
54 and over	19	8	26	10
Total percent	100	100	100	100
Number	628	147	337	231
x^2 probability	<.001		<.001	
	$(x^2 = 20, df - 4)$		$(x^2 = 23)$	
Education				
Less than high school	51	39	33	19
High school completion	34	38	40	47
Some college/college completion	15	23	27	34
Total percent	100	100	100	100
Number	625	148	335	231
x^2 probability	<.05		<.01	
	$(x^2 = 8, df = 2)$		$(x^2 = 13)$	
Family income (dollars)				
0-2,999	20	7	3	0
3,000-5,999	51	38	9	3
6,000-9,999	22	42	16	10
10,000-14,999	4	12	26	24
15,000 or more	3	1	46	63
Total percent	100	100	100	100
Number	611	145	306	225
x^2 probability	<.001		<.001	
	$(x^2 = 47, df = 4)$		$(x^2 = 27)$	

Table A-2
Converted Family Income by Employment Status
(percent)

	1957		1976	
Family *Income*[a]	*Home* *Wives* *(n = 611)*	*Market* *Wives* *(n = 145)*	*Home* *Wives* *(n = 306)*	*Market* *Wives* *(n = 225)*
Low	20	7	18	8
Middle	51	38	36	29
High	29	55	45	63
Total	100	100	100	100

Note: Because income categorizations were not the same in each survey, conversion represents an approximation.

[a]Family income (dollars):

	1957	1976
Low	0-2,999	0-7,999
Middle	3,000-5,999	8,000-14,999
High	6,000 and over	15,000 and over

Table A-3
Mother's Employment Status by Age of Youngest Child
(percent)

Age of *Youngest* *Child* *(years)*	1957		1976	
	Home *Wives* *(n = 560)*	*Labor* *Wives* *(n = 107)*	*Home* *Wives* *(n = 315)*	*Labor* *Wives* *(n = 177)*
0-5	47	17	32	24
6-12	19	37	25	35
13-18	7	20	11	16
19 and over	26	26	32	25
Total	100	100	100	100
x^2 probability	<.001		.01	
	$(x^2 = 48, df = 3)$		$(x^2 = 11)$	

Table A-4
Occupational Distribution for Labor-Market Wives, 1957 and 1976
(percent)

Occupation Category[a]	1957 (n = 145)	1976 (n = 230)
1. Includes laborers, service workers	10	17
2. Includes crafts, operatives	20	12
3. Includes clerical, sales	46	42
4. Includes professionals, managers	24	29
Total	100	100
x^2 probability	not significant	

[a]Occupations listed are intended to exemplify the types of occupations found in each category and do not indicate an exhaustive listing.

Appendix B
Working Wives'
Preference for
Other Work

Table B-1

Working Wives' Preference for Other Work by Education and Occupation, 1957 and 1976

	Working Wives Who Prefer Other Work[a]			
	1957		1976	
	Percent	*Number*	*Percent*	*Number*
Education				
Less than high school	21	43	32	44
High school	29	38	44	108
College	25	24	42	78
Occupational Level				
1. Includes laborers, service workers	17	12	31	39
2. Includes craftsmen, operatives	20	15	43	18
3. Includes clericals, sales	29	51	49	96
4. Includes professionals, managers	20	25	36	66

[a]Does not include those preferring to be full-time housewives.

Appendix C
Correlation Matrix for
Working Wives

Table C-1

Correlation Matrix for Demographic Categorical Variables for
Labor-Market Wives, 1957 and 1976

		Tau-Beta Correlations			
Year	Education	Family Income	Occupation	Age	Age of Youngest Child
1957					
Education	1.000				
Family income	.253[a]	1.000			
Occupation	.415[a]	.202[a]	1.000		
Age	−.047	−.099[a]	.040	1.000	
Age of youngest child	−.185[a]	−.080	−.063	.6088[a]	1.000
1976					
Education	1.000				
Family income	.239[a]	1.000			
Occupation	.492[a]	.236[a]	1.000		
Age	−.230[a]	−.088[a]	−.064[a]	1.000	
Age of youngest child	−.113[a]	−.121[a]	.030	.723[a]	1.000

[a]Denotes statistical significance.

Bibliography

Andrews, Frank; Morgan, James; Sonquist, John; and Klem, Laura. *Multiple Classification Analysis.* 2d ed. Ann Arbor, Mich.: Institute for Social Research, 1973.

Beckett, Joyce O. "Working Wives: A Racial Comparison." *Social Work* 21 (November, 1976):463-471.

Bentson, Margaret. "The Political Economy of Women's Liberation." *Voices from Women's Liberation*, edited by Leslie B. Tanner. New York: New American Library, 1970.

Bernard, Jessie. *Marriage and Family among Negroes.* Englewood Cliffs, N.J.: Prentice-Hall, Inc., 1966.

Blalock, Hubert M. *Social Statistics.* 2d ed. New York: McGraw-Hill Book Company, 1972.

Blood, Robert O., Jr. "Long Range Causes and Consequences of the Employment of Married Women." *Journal of Marriage and the Family* 27 (February, 1965):43-47.

Bowen, William, and Finegan, T. Aldrich. *The Economics of Labor Force Participation.* Princeton, N.J.: Princeton University Press, 1969.

Broverman, Inge K.; Vogel, Susan R.; Broverman, Donald M.; Clarkson, Frank E.; and Rosenkrantz, Paul S. "Sex Role Stereotypes: A Current Appraisal." *Journal of Social Issues* vol. 28 no. 2 (1972):59-76.

Burke, Ronald J., and Weir, Tamara. "Relationship of Wives' Employment Status to Husband, Wife and Pair Satisfaction and Performance." *Journal of Marriage and the Family* 38 (May 1976):279-287.

Cain, Glenn. *Married Women in the Labor Force.* Chicago: University of Chicago Press, 1966.

Cantril, Hadley. *Public Opinion, 1935-46.* Princeton, N.J.: Princeton University Press, 1951.

Chafe, William H. *The American Woman: Her Changing Social, Economic, and Political Roles, 1920-1970.* New York: Oxford University Press, 1972.

_____ . "Looking Backward in Order to Look Forward: Women, Work and Social Values in America." *Women and the American Economy*, edited by Juanita M. Kreps. Englewood Cliffs, N.J.: Prentice-Hall, Inc., 1976.

Clinch, Mary. "Phenomenon of the Working Wife." (Abstract). *Marriage and Family Living* 19 (1957):298.

Coser, Rose L., and Rokoff, Gerald. "Women in the Occupational World: Social Disruption and Conflict." *Social Problems* 18 (Spring 1971):535-553.

Darley, Susan. "Big-Time Career for the Little Woman: A Dual-Role Dilemma." *Journal of Social Issues* 32 (Summer 1976):85-98.

Davis, J.A. "Hierarchical Models for Significance Tests in Multivariate Contingency Tables: An Exegesis of Goodman's Recent Papers." *Sociological Methodology, 1973-1974*, edited by Herbert L. Costner. San Francisco: Jossey-Bass, 1974.

Day, Lincoln H. "Status Implications of the Employment of Married Women." *American Journal of Economics and Sociology* 20 (July 1961):391-397.

Deckard, Barbara. *The Women's Movement: Political, Socioeconomic, and Psychological Issues.* New York: Harper and Row, 1975.

Degler, Carl N. "The Changing Place of Women in America." *Daedalus* 93 (Spring 1964):653-670.

Duncan, Otis; Schuman, Howard; and Duncan, Beverly. *Social Changes in a Metropolitan Community.* New York: Russell Sage Foundation, 1973.

Durand, John D. "Married Women in the Labor Force." *American Journal of Sociology* 52 (November, 1946):217-223.

Epstein, Cynthia F. *Woman's Place.* Los Angeles: University of California Press, 1970.

Farmer, Helen, and Bohn, Martin. "Home-Career Conflict Redirection and the Level of Career Interest in Women." *Journal of Counseling Psychology* 17 (May, 1970):228-232.

Feld, Sheila. "Feelings of Adjustment." *The Employed Mother in America*, edited by F. Ivan Nye and Lois W. Hoffman. Chicago: Rand McNally and Co., 1963.

Ferree, Myra Marx. "Working-Class Jobs: Housework and Paid Work as Sources of Satisfaction." *Social Problems* 22 (April, 1975):431-441.

Fortune. "The Fortune Survey: Women in America." 34 (August, 1946):5ff.

Friedan, Betty. *The Feminine Mystique.* New York: Dell Publishing Co., 1963.

Gallup, George H. *The Gallup Poll: Public Opinion 1935-1971.* 3 vols. New York: Random House, 1972.

Glazer, Nona. "Housework: A Review Essay." *Woman in a Man-Made World*, edited by Nona Glazer and Helen Waehrer. Chicago: Rand McNally, 1977.

Glenn, H.M. "Attitudes of Women Regarding Gainful Employment of Married Women." *Journal of Home Economics* 51 (August, 1959):247-252.

Gold, David. "Statistical Significance and Substantive Significance." *The American Sociologist* 4 (February, 1969):42-46.

Gurin, Gerald; Veroff, Joseph; and Feld, Sheila. *Americans View Their Mental Health.* New York: Basic Books, Inc., 1960.

Haber, Sheldon. "Trends in Work Rates of White Females: 1890-1950." *Industrial and Labor Relations Review*, 26 (July, 1973):1122-1134.

Hatch, Mary, and Hatch, David L. "Problems of Married Working Women as Presented by Three Popular Working Women's Magazines." *Social Forces* 37 (December, 1958):148-153.

Hayghe, Howard. "Families and the Rise of Working Wives—an Overview." *Monthly Labor Review* 99 (May, 1976):12-19.

Hedges, Janice. "Women Workers and Manpower Demands in the 1970s." *Monthly Labor Review* 93 (June, 1970):19-29.

Hedges, Janice, and Barnett, Jeanne K. "Working Women and the Division of Household Tasks." *Monthly Labor Review* (April, 1972):9-13.

Helson, Ravenna. "Changing Image of the Career Woman." *Journal of Social Issues* vol. 28, no. 2 (1972):33-46.

Hochschild, Arlie. "A Review of Sex-Role Research." *Changing Women in a Changing Society*, edited by Joan Huber. Chicago: University of Chicago Press, 1973.

Hoffman, Lois W. "Effects of Maternal Employment on the Child—A Review of the Research." *Developmental Psychology* 10 (March, 1974):204-228.

Hoffman, Lois W., and Nye, F. Ivan. *Working Mothers.* San Francisco: Jossey-Bass Publishers, 1974.

Josselyn, I.M., and Goldman, R.S. "Should Mothers Work?" *Social Service Review* 23 (March, 1949):74-87.

Kanter, Rosabeth Moss. *Men and Women of the Corporation.* New York: Basic Books, Inc., 1977a.

_____. *Work and Family in the U.S.: A Critical Review and Agenda for Research and Policy.* New York: Russell Sage Foundation, 1977b.

Katz, Irwin, and Gurin, Patricia, eds. *Race and the Social Sciences.* New York: Basic Books, 1969.

Keller, Suzanne. "The Female Role: Constants and Changes." *Women in Therapy*, edited by Violet Franks and Vasanti Burtle. New York: Brunner/Mazel, 1974.

King, Mae C. "Oppression and Power: The Unique Status of the Black Woman in the American Political System." *Social Science Quarterly* 56 (June, 1975):116-128.

Kiser, Clyde W.; Grabill, Wilson H.; and Campbell, Arthur A. *Trends and Variations in Fertility in the United States.* Cambridge, Mass.: Harvard University Press, 1968.

Kluckhohn, Florence. "Cultural Factors in Social Work Practice and Education." *Social Service Review* 25 (March, 1951):38-47.

Knudsen, D.D. "Declining Status of Women: Popular Myths and the Failure of Functionalist Thought." *Social Forces* 45 (December, 1969):183-193.

Kohlberg, L. "A Cognitive Development Analysis of Children's Sex-Role Concepts and Attitudes." *The Development of Sex Differences*, edited by E.E. Maccoby. Stanford, Calif.: Stanford University Press, 1966.

Komarovsky, Mirra. "Cultural Contradictions and Sex Roles." *American Journal of Sociology* 52 (November, 1946):184-189.

_____. *Blue Collar Marriage.* New York: Vintage Books, 1967.

Kreps, Juanita. "Do All Women Want to Work?" *The Future of the Family*, edited by Louise Howe. New York: Touchstone, 1972.

Kreps, Juanita, and Leaper, R. John. "Home Work, Market Work, and the Allocation of Time." *Women and the American Economy*, edited by Juanita Kreps. Englewood Cliffs, N.J.: Prentice-Hall, 1976.

Ladner, Joyce A. *Tomorrow's Tomorrow. The Black Woman.* Garden City, N.Y.: Doubleday and Co., 1972.

LaRue, Linda. "The Black Movement and Women's Liberation." *Black Scholar* 1 (May, 1970):36-42.

Laws, Judith Long. "A Feminist View of Marital Adjustment Literature: The Rape of the Locke." *Journal of Marriage and the Family* 33 (August, 1971):483-516.

Lebergott, Stanley. "Labor Force and Employment Trends." *Indicators of Social Change*, edited by Eleanor B. Sheldon and Wilbert E. Moore. New York: Russell Sage Foundation, 1968.

Lifton, Robert J., ed. *The Woman in America.* Boston: Houghton Mifflin Co., 1965.

Locke, Harvey J., and Mackeprang, Muriel. "Marital Adjustment of the Employed Wife." *American Journal of Sociology* 54 (May, 1949):536-539.

Lopata, Helena Z. *Occupation: Housewife.* New York: Oxford University Press, 1971.

Lundberg, Ferdinand, and Farnham, Marynia. *Modern Woman: The Lost Sex.* New York: Harper and Brothers, 1947.

Lyle, Jerolyn R., and Ross, Jane L. *Women in Industry.* Lexington, Mass.: D.C. Heath and Co., 1973.

Mainardi, Pat. "The Politics of Housework." *Sisterhood is Powerful,* edited by Robin Morgan. New York: Vintage Books, 1970.

Maret-Havens, Elizabeth. "Developing an Index to Measure Female Labor Force Attachment." *Monthly Labor Review* 100 (May, 1977):35-38.

Mason, Karen; Czajka, John; and Arber, Sara. "Change in U.S. Women's Sex-Role Attitudes, 1964-1974." *American Sociological Review* 41 (August, 1976):573-596.

Mayo, Julie. "The New Black Feminism: A Minority Report." *Contemporary Sexual Behavior: Critical Issues in the 1970s,* edited by Joseph Zubin and John Money. Baltimore: Johns Hopkins University Press, 1973.

Mead, Margaret. *Male and Female.* New York: William Morrow and Co., 1949.

Mischel, W. "Sex-Typing and Socialization." *Carmichael's Manual of Child Psychology,* vol. 2. 3d ed., edited by P.H. Mussen. New York: John Wiley and Sons, 1970.

Miyahira, Sarah D. "Marriage and the Employment of Women." *Emerging Woman: Career Analysis and Outlooks.* Edited by Samuel H. Osipow. Columbus: Charles E. Merrill, 1975.

Nevill, Dorothy, and Damico, Sandra. "Role Conflict in Women as a Function of Marital Status." *Human Relations* 38 (July, 1975):487-497.

Nolan, F.I., and Tuttle, D.H. "Certain Practices, Satisfactions, and Difficulties in Families with Employed Homemakers." Bulletin no. 655, Agricultural Experiment Station, Pennsylvania State University, 1959.

Nye, F. Ivan. "Employment Status of Mothers and Marital Conflict, Permanence and Happiness." *Social Problems* 6 (Winter, 1958):260-267.

_____. "Personal Satisfactions." *The Employed Mother in America,* edited by F. Ivan Nye and Lois W. Hoffman. Chicago: Rand McNally and Co., 1963a.

_____ . "Recreation and Community." *The Employed Mother in America*, edited by F. Ivan Nye and Lois W. Hoffman. Chicago: Rand McNally and Co., 1963b.

_____ . "Effects on Mother." *Working Mothers*, edited by Lois Hoffman and F. Ivan Nye. San Francisco: Jossey-Bass Publishers, 1974.

Nye, F. Ivan, and Hoffman, Lois W., eds. *The Employed Mother in America*. Chicago: Rand McNally and Co., 1963.

Oakley, Ann. *Woman's Work*. New York: Pantheon Books, 1974.

_____ . *The Sociology of Housework*. New York: Pantheon Books, 1975.

Oppenheimer, Valeria K. *The Female Labor Force in the United States: Demographic and Economic Factors Governing Its Growth and Changing Composition*. Population Monograph Series, no. 5. Berkeley, Calif.: University of California, 1970.

_____ . "Demographic Influence on Female Employment and the Status of Women." *Changing Women in a Changing Society*, edited by Joan Huber. Chicago: University of Chicago Press, 1973.

Orden, Susan R., and Bradburn, Norman M. "Working Wives and Marriage Happiness." *American Journal of Sociology* 74 (January, 1969):392-407.

O'Reilly, Jane. "The Housewife's Moment of Truth." *The First Ms. Reader*, edited by Francine Klagsburn. New York: Warner Communications Company, 1973.

Polk, Barbara. "Women's Liberation: Movement for Equality." *Toward a Sociology of Women*, edited by Constantina Safilios-Rothschild. Toronto: Xerox College Publishing, 1972.

Powell, K.S. "Maternal Employment in Relation to Family Life." *Marriage and Family Living* 23 (November, 1961):350-355.

Rice, Joy, and Rice, David. "Implications of the Women's Liberation Movement for Psychotherapy." *American Journal of Psychiatry* 130 (February, 1973):191-196.

Robinson, John P. *How Americans Use Time*. New York: Praeger Publishers, 1977.

Rossi, Alice M. "Equality between the Sexes: An Immodest Proposal." *Daedalus* 93 (Spring, 1964):98-143.

Safilios-Rothschild, Constantina. "Towards the Conceptualization and Measurement of Work Commitment." *Human Relations* 24 (1971):489-493.

_____, ed. *Toward a Sociology of Women.* Toronto: Xerox College Publishing, 1972.

Schiffler, Richard J. "Demographic and Social Factors in Women's Work Lives." *Emerging Woman: Career Analysis and Outlook,* edited by Samuel H. Osipow. Columbus, Ohio: Charles E. Merrill, 1975.

Shaffer, Juliet Popper. "Defining and Testing Hypotheses in Multi-dimensional Contingency Tables." *Psychological Bulletin* 79 (February, 1973):127-141.

Siegel, Alberta E., and Haas, Miriam B. "The Working Mother: A Review of Research." *Child Development* 34 (September, 1963):513-542.

Smuts, Robert W. *Women and Work in America.* New York: Columbia University Press, 1959.

Staples, Robert. *The Black Woman in America.* Chicago: Nelson-Hall Publishers, 1973.

Stevens, Barbara. "The Psychotherapist and Woman's Liberation." *Social Work* 16 (July, 1971):12-18.

Stolz, L. "Effects of Maternal Employment on Children: Evidence from Research." *Child Development* 31 (February, 1960): 749-782.

Sweet, James A. *Women in the Labor Force.* New York: Seminar Press, 1973.

Szymanski, Albert. "Race, Sex, and the U.S. Working Class." *Social Problems* 21 (June, 1974):706-725.

Tsuchigane, Robert, and Doge, Norton. *Economic Discrimination against Women in the United States.* Lexington, Mass.: D.C. Heath and Company, 1974.

U.S. Bureau of the Census. *Employment Status and Work Experience.* 1970 Census of the Population. Subject Report 6A, 1973.

_____. *Population of the United States, Trends and Prospects: 1950-1990.* Current Population Reports, series P-23, no. 49. Washington, D.C.: Government Printing Office, 1974a.

_____. *The Social and Economic Status of the Black Population in the United States, 1973.* Current Population Reports, series P-23, no. 48. Washington, D.C.: Government Printing Office, 1974b.

U.S. Department of Labor, Women's Bureau. *Effective Industrial Use of Women in the Defense Program.* Washington, D.C.: Government Printing Office, 1944.

_____. *Women's Occupations through Seven Decades*. No. 218. Washington, D.C.: Government Printing Office, 1947.

_____. *1952 Handbook of Facts on Women Workers*, Bulletin 242. Washington, D.C.: Government Printing Office, 1952.

_____. *1975 Handbook on Women Workers*. Bulletin 297. Washington, D.C.: Government Printing Office, 1975.

Van Dusen, Roxann A. and Sheldon, Eleanor B. "Changing Status of American Women: A Life Cycle Perspective." *American Psychologist* 31 (February, 1976):106-116.

Vanek, Joann. "Keeping Busy: Time Spent in Housework, United States, 1920-1970." Unpublished Ph.D. dissertation, University of Michigan, 1973.

_____. "Time Spent in Housework." *Scientific American*, 231 (November, 1974):116-120.

Veroff, Joseph, and Feld, Sheila. *Marriage and Work in America*. New York: Van Nostrand Reinhold Company, 1970.

Waite, Linda. "Working Wives: 1940-1960." *American Sociological Review* 41 (February, 1976):65-80.

Waldman, Elizabeth. "Changes in the Labor Force Activity of Women." *Monthly Labor Review* 93 (June, 1970):10-18.

Weaver, Charles N. "What Women Want in a Job." *The Personnel Administrator* 22 (June, 1977):66-71.

Weaver, Charles N. and Holmes, Sandra L. "Comparative Study of the Work Satisfaction of Females with Full-Time Employment and Full-Time Housekeeping." *Journal of Applied Psychology* 60 (February, 1975):117-118.

Weil, Mildred W. "Analysis of Factors Influencing Married Women's Actual or Planned Work Participation." *American Sociological Review* 26 (February, 1961):91-96.

Weiss, Robert S. and Samelson, Nancy. "Social Roles of American Women: Their Contribution to a Sense of Usefulness and Importance." *Marriage and Family Living* 20 (November, 1958): 358-366.

Willie, Charles V. "Marginality and Social Change." *Society* 12 (July/August, 1975):10-13.

Winch, Robert F. and Campbell, Donald T. "Proof? No. Evidence? Yes. The Significance of Tests of Significance." *The American Sociologist* 4 (May, 1969):140-143.

Author Index

Subject Index

Age, 19; of housewives planning to work, 51, 52; and labor-force participation, 3-4; and work commitment, 31, 49-50

Age of youngest child, 19, 21; and labor-force participation, 6-7; and opinion of housework, 45-46, 47-48; and self-perceptions, 71-73; and work commitment, 31-32, 33

Americans View Their Mental Health, 16

Attitude toward marriage and children, 62-64

Attitudinal variables, 18

Black wives, 10, 84-85

Categorical variables, 19

Child-care facilities, 6, 7, 81-82

Clerical and sales workers, 28-30

Community activities, 82

Demographic variables, 18

Economic needs, 23-24; of housewives planning to work, 52, 55-56

Education, 19-20, 84; of housewives planning to work, 51, 52-54; and opinion of housework, 46, 49-50; and preference for other work, 28-30; and work commitment, 31, 32, 34, 37-38

Ego satisfaction, 37-38, 55. *See also* Self-actualization

Family size: and labor-force participation, 7

Free-time hypothesis, 7-8

Housewives, 41-58, 82-84; planning to work, 50-56, 57-58

Housework, 41-44, 83; opinion of, 44-50, 57-58

Income, family, 20-21; of housewives planning to work, 52; and opinion of housework, 46, 48-49; and work commitment, 32-33, 35

Job satisfaction, 25-26

Labor-force participation: as a "social problem," 10-11; trends, 2-4

Labor-saving devices, 7-8, 58

Life happiness, 60; and work status, 73-74

Marital status: and labor-force participation, 2-3

Marriage and Work in America, 16

Maternal deprivation, 11, 24

Occupation, 20; and preference for other work, 28-30; and work commitment, 31, 32

Predictor variables, 19

Preference for housework or another job, 27-30

Public attitudes, 23-24, 74

Push and pull theories, 4-8

Reference groups, work/family, 81

Research methodology, 16-22

Role inadequacy, feelings of, 65-69

Role performance, 59-60; and role perceptions, 61-69

Self-actualization, 46, 54, 61, 83. *See also* Ego satisfaction

Self-perceptions, 60-61; and age of youngest child, 71-73; and work status, 69-73

Sex discrimination, 80-81

Sex-role ideology, 8-11

Significance, statistical/substantive, 18-19

About the Author

Alfreda P. Iglehart received the Master of Social Work from Our Lady of the Lake University and the Ph.D. in social work and sociology from the University of Michigan. She is a postdoctoral fellow with the Survey Research Center, Institute for Social Research, and a lecturer with the School of Social Work at the University of Michigan. In addition to wives and work, her current research activities include study of the correlates of female criminality.